Ethical Issues in the 21st Century

Ethics

Past, Present and Future Perspectives

ETHICAL ISSUES IN THE 21ST CENTURY

Additional books in this series can be found on Nova's website under the Series tab.

Additional e-books in this series can be found on Nova's website under the eBooks tab.

ETHICAL ISSUES IN THE 21ST CENTURY

ETHICS

PAST, PRESENT AND FUTURE PERSPECTIVES

MILES VENTURA
EDITOR

Copyright © 2018 by Nova Science Publishers, Inc.

All rights reserved. No part of this book may be reproduced, stored in a retrieval system or transmitted in any form or by any means: electronic, electrostatic, magnetic, tape, mechanical photocopying, recording or otherwise without the written permission of the Publisher.

We have partnered with Copyright Clearance Center to make it easy for you to obtain permissions to reuse content from this publication. Simply navigate to this publication's page on Nova's website and locate the "Get Permission" button below the title description. This button is linked directly to the title's permission page on copyright.com. Alternatively, you can visit copyright.com and search by title, ISBN, or ISSN.

For further questions about using the service on copyright.com, please contact:
Copyright Clearance Center
Phone: +1-(978) 750-8400   Fax: +1-(978) 750-4470   E-mail: info@copyright.com.

NOTICE TO THE READER

The Publisher has taken reasonable care in the preparation of this book, but makes no expressed or implied warranty of any kind and assumes no responsibility for any errors or omissions. No liability is assumed for incidental or consequential damages in connection with or arising out of information contained in this book. The Publisher shall not be liable for any special, consequential, or exemplary damages resulting, in whole or in part, from the readers' use of, or reliance upon, this material. Any parts of this book based on government reports are so indicated and copyright is claimed for those parts to the extent applicable to compilations of such works.

Independent verification should be sought for any data, advice or recommendations contained in this book. In addition, no responsibility is assumed by the publisher for any injury and/or damage to persons or property arising from any methods, products, instructions, ideas or otherwise contained in this publication.

This publication is designed to provide accurate and authoritative information with regard to the subject matter covered herein. It is sold with the clear understanding that the Publisher is not engaged in rendering legal or any other professional services. If legal or any other expert assistance is required, the services of a competent person should be sought. FROM A DECLARATION OF PARTICIPANTS JOINTLY ADOPTED BY A COMMITTEE OF THE AMERICAN BAR ASSOCIATION AND A COMMITTEE OF PUBLISHERS.

Additional color graphics may be available in the e-book version of this book.

Library of Congress Cataloging-in-Publication Data

ISBN: 978-1-53613-533-6

Published by Nova Science Publishers, Inc. † New York

CONTENTS

Preface		**vii**
Chapter 1	Ethics and the Challenges of the Contemporary World (Selected Problems) *Anetta Breczko and Agata Breczko*	**1**
Chapter 2	Monism, Dualism, and Supervenience: A Debate on Distributive Justice *Benedict S. B. Chan*	**25**
Chapter 3	The Importance of Establishing Ethics Committees within the Health Sector *Jorge Morales Pedraza*	**45**
Chapter 4	The Convergence of Technologies in Healthcare: New Challenges for Bioethics *Pamela Tozzo and Luciana Caenazzo*	**71**
Index		**87**

PREFACE

In *Ethics: Past, Present and Future Perspectives*, the authors open by making a characterization of ethics viewed as a domain of philosophy. They present traditional approaches to ethics and point out the importance of general and special ethics in contemporary philosophical discourse. A conclusion is drawn that a clear need arises to discuss the so-called "new ethics", one which is removed from the schematic thinking on "good" and "evil." The following chapter discusses Nagel's dualism and Murphy's monism in depth. Both of them limit their discussions to distributive justice, but they admit that their views can apply to a more general discussion of the relationship between politics and morality. The authors suggest that supervenience is the key to solve this problem, using it as a standard to evaluate arguments from both sides, and then arguing that a supervenience relationship between politics and morality would be the third and better position than both dualism and monism. This collection examines ethics committees in hospitals, clinics, and other medical and research medical institutions within the public and private sector. An ethics committee is a group of individuals formed to protect the interests of patients and address moral issues within the health sector in many countries, consisting of different healthcare professionals and non-medical members. The following chapter discusses the convergence of technologies and scientific disciplines: singly, each of them has a large potential to change society and mankind, but combined they represent a more powerful source for even bigger changes. The increasingly widespread use of digital recording in administrative, commercial and social networks is opening up new and unpredictable scenario which might also influence the definition of disease in a digital society. The authors propose that by developing appropriate algorithms, it would be possible to identify subsets of the population at higher risk of developing diseases, to ascertain whether distances between homes and drugstores or hospitals influence people's health profiles, to see whether the characteristics shared by Facebook friends influence their individual health profiles, and so on.

Chapter 1 - In this chapter, the authors make a characterization of ethics viewed as a domain of philosophy. The authors present traditional approaches to ethics and point out the importance of general and special ethics in contemporary philosophical discourse. The authors also draw attention to the multiplicity of moral systems and the ambiguity and variability of axiological criteria in pluralistic societies. The authors mention the risks inherent in European culture, closely related to the crisis of liberal democracy, the ideology of multiculturalism and postmodernism, and due to the existing discordance between normative and descriptive ethics. Afterward, the authors emphasize the importance of applied and situational ethics which both are complementary to traditional approaches. Finally, the authors conclude that a clear need arises to discuss the so-called "new ethics," one which is removed from the schematic thinking on "good" and "evil."

Chapter 2 - What is the relationship between politics and morality? In this chapter, the author discusses Nagel's dualism and Murphy's monism in depth. Both of them limit their discussions to distributive justice, but they admit that their views can apply to a more general discussion of the relationship between politics and morality. On one

Preface

hand, Nagel argues that distributive justice can only be assured by nation-states because only states have *associative responsibility*; associative responsibility does not apply to any particular individual. On the other hand, Murphy argues that the authors should assure justice by both institutions and individuals, and only monism could explain why a person should act to assure justice in non-ideal situations. Both arguments have strengths and weaknesses. Nagel tells us how important sovereignty is, and Murphy tells us how important it is to assure justice. Nevertheless, Nagel fails to explain why individuals are not required to assure justice, and Murphy fails to explain how principles of justice can apply to individuals. The most important problem is that they do not have the same standard to evaluate and justify both positions. Although both of them have their own reasons to support their own view, it is unclear how they can refute the opposite side. The author suggests that supervenience is the key to solve this problem. The author uses supervenience as a standard to evaluate arguments from both sides, and then argue that a supervenience relationship between politics and morality would be the third and better position than both dualism and monism.

Chapter 3 - Most hospitals, clinics, and other medical and research medical institutions within the public and private sector established in different countries, are now required to have an ethics committee. In the US and in several other countries, many of these ethics committees provide an ethics consultation service as well. An ethics committee is a group of individuals formed to protect the interests of patients and address moral issues within the health sector in many countries, consisting of different healthcare professionals and non-medical members. Its main responsibilities are to protect the rights, safety, and well-being of human subjects involved in a clinical trial, to provide public assurance of that protection by, among other things, expressing an opinion on the clinical trial protocol to be used, the suitability of the investigators involved in the trial and the adequacy of the facilities, and on the methods and documents to be used to inform trial subjects and obtain their informed consent.

Chapter 4 - During the last two decades new forms and types of technologies have emerged: some examples include nanotechnology, neuroscience/neurotechnology, and many converging technologies that combine bio- and nanotechnology with physical sciences. In this chapter the authors will address some bioethical issues raised by the convergence of these new technologies. The technological convergence reinforces the development of the technologies involved, creating new application domains by their combination, with an important influence in medical sciences. In this developing field, the authors can distinguish among different pathways, but particularly in the field of public health they see different emerging projects regarding record-linkage between *Big Data* archives of various origins (commercial, economic, institutional, social networks, etc.) resulting in the definition of subsets of the population to be considered at higher risk of developing a particular disease, and record-linkage between electronic administrative health archives, which could be processed using disease-specific algorithms to identify individuals with disease in a population. The increasingly widespread use of digital recording in administrative, commercial and social networks is opening up new and unpredictable scenario which might also influence the definition of disease in a digital society. Some Authors have addressed this issue, examining the feasibility of record linking between health-related archives and other electronic archives such as Facebook, Twitter, blogs, online shopping habits, GPS recordings of individual mobility, personal devices monitoring physical exercise, and so on. By developing appropriate algorithms, it would be possible to identify subsets of the population at higher risk of developing diseases, to ascertain whether distances between homes and drugstores or hospitals influence people's health profiles, to see whether the characteristics shared by Facebook friends influence their individual health profiles, and so on. The possibilities related to the use of this data are limitless, and inevitably give rise to

Preface xi

ethical aspects related to the value of data, privacy concerns, consent, and population health priorities and related needs, management of prevention campaigns, public health intervention planning and resource allocation.

In: Ethics
Editor: Miles Ventura

ISBN: 978-1-53613-533-6
© 2018 Nova Science Publishers, Inc.

Chapter 1

ETHICS AND THE CHALLENGES OF THE CONTEMPORARY WORLD (SELECTED PROBLEMS)

Anetta Breczko and Agata Breczko[†]*
[1]Department of Theory of Law and Philosophy of Law,
University of Białystok, Białystok, Poland
[2]Institute of Economic Research
UNAM, Mexico City, Mexico

ABSTRACT

In this chapter, we make a characterization of ethics viewed as a domain of philosophy. We present traditional approaches to ethics and point out the importance of general and special ethics in contemporary philosophical discourse. We also draw attention to the multiplicity of moral systems and the ambiguity and variability of axiological criteria in pluralistic societies. We mention the risks inherent in European culture,

---

* Corresponding Author Email: breczko@uwb.edu.pl.
[†] Corresponding Author Email: agata.breczko@comunidad.unam.mx.

closely related to the crisis of liberal democracy, the ideology of multiculturalism and postmodernism, and due to the existing discordance between normative and descriptive ethics. Afterward, we emphasize the importance of applied and situational ethics which both are complementary to traditional approaches. Finally, we conclude that a clear need arises to discuss the so-called "new ethics," one which is removed from the schematic thinking on "good" and "evil."

Keywords: ethics, morality, professional deontology, situationism, virtue ethics and role models, Christian ethics

INTRODUCTION

Ethics, the study of morality, constitutes one of the domains of philosophy which currently contains metaphysical, ontological, epistemological and axiological considerations. On the basis of ethical reflection, the answer to the following question becomes vital: why do people make some, and not other, moral choices? There is no simple answer, considering that behaviours that were at some point seen as "good" can become "evil incarnate," when the "moral bill" is tallied up by history. And although it is commonly acknowledged that it is precisely morality which makes us "civilised human beings," while the concept of "culture" signifies socially transmitted standards of "good" behaviour, we still do not know from where the "square root of evil," terrifying in its immensity and characterising modern societies, originates (Schmidt-Salomon, 2013: 63).

The liberal, civilised Europe of the 20th century has turned out to be a "laboratory of rape" (Traverso, 2003). An immense "barbaric potential" was unleashed at that time. Nothing would seem to indicate that this "laboratory" has ceased to exist in the 21st century. On the contrary. Already at its very start, we have seen examples of barbaric practices: regional conflicts, ongoing wars, the migratory crisis, terrorism, social divisions, religious fundamentalism, spread of nationalist ideologies etc.

Ethics and the Challenges of the Contemporary World 3

Furthermore, in the context of globalisation - coupled with local cultural diversity in today's multicultural world - traditional approaches in ethics turn out to be insufficient. There is a clear need for a new and more "open" look at the criteria defining "good" and "evil," taking into account cultural differences that exist in dynamic and "mixed" human societies.

The simultaneous convergence and divergence of cultures (moral and legal) contributes to the fact that the discussions on morality are becoming more and more complex. The assumptions of general ethics no longer constitute a self-contained basis for solving the moral dilemmas of the 21st century. In ethical discourse, applied and situational ethics are beginning to play a significant role. They become complementary to traditional approaches, dealing with ethical problems by going far beyond the framework of culturally-rooted notions of "good" and "evil."

It could be that these "dark forces" which appear among mankind are the result of an unconscious, immature relationship with a human potential full of humanitarianism. It could even be that the concept of evil itself is an absurdity which has taken root in our minds, which should be freed of social and genetic factors so as to build a new ethics, filled with "true humanity."

Maybe, that "square root of evil" - inseparable from human nature and inevitable while making specific moral choices - could at least be lessened, by providing adequate education on ethics.

WHY DO PEOPLE MAKE SPECIFIC MORAL CHOICES AND WHAT IS TRUTH?

In order to recognise the aforementioned "true humanity," one should first determine what truth is. It turns out that the classical definition of truth, understood as the conformity of judgements with reality, does not apply well to normative statements. In such a case, a more adequate concept would appear to be that grouped under the terms: "coherent, "conciliatory" or "agreed truth." In these conceptions of "truth" (here, the quotes are in fact indispensable), it is that which a given society has accepted as the truth during its civilisational evolution. For this type of "truth," there exists no scientific proof. It is useful to note that in the modern world many such "truths" function alongside each other (with each being culturally-determined). Archaic thought patterns (the perduring schematic opposition between "good" and "evil") lead to the attribution of the stigmata of evil to "others," "dissenters," "opponents," that is those originating from different cultures (and who do not share the dominant values). This leads to an escalation of violence (Kołakowski, 2014: 95-110).

Paradoxically, it is precisely this pluralism of values, and the freedom of the individual – treated as the inalienable foundation of a democratic state – which is implicated in people "losing their bearings" and the current crisis of values. The assumptions behind multiculturalism (linked to the hope of a harmonious co-existence between various minorities) appear to be inadequate when faced with reality (Sykuna, 2009: 189-204). Today, refugees have become the symbol of the "redundant society" which G. Agamben called *homo sacer* (Agamben, 2008). This "open" world, up till now democratic, has started to build walls and implement borders, while limiting individual freedoms (and the related possibility of making autonomous moral decisions) in the name of public safety. An ever more thorough control and surveillance of society (including the most intimate spheres of private life) is made possible thanks to new monitoring techniques; technologies which R. Braidotti has called post-anthropocentric (Braidotti, 2014: 248). Increasingly, there are doubts about whether humanism can be reconciled with moral relativism (Einstein, 1994: 144). These doubts increase with the crisis of liberal democracy as well as that of the ideologies of multiculturalism and postmodernism.

Ethics and the Challenges of the Contemporary World 5

The contemporary considerations of ethicists concentrate on the numerous threats to European culture, posed by totalitarian practices in their many guises: philosophical, religious or political. One of the most important questions would appear to be the role of ethics as applied to the concept of individual freedom. Within European civilisation, we search for themes which: "would allow us to hope that they can oppose both the barbarity endangering it, and that which it produces itself" (Amsterdamski, 1987: 13-14).

Today, the hope which postmodernists clung to until recently, namely that of a "world without ethics" and a "morality without a code," appears to have misplaced. Such ideas were expressed in the works of Z. Bauman (Bauman, 1995: 147-159). L. Kołakowski also referred to such concepts (Kołakowski, 2000: 137-175). It seems improbable that these visions of a "morality without a code" could become reality in the near future. That this "liberation" from moral codes is impossible is illustrated by the ever greater juridification of the domains relating to morality (e.g., human procreation or sexuality in general). At the basis of this lies a specific manner of defining "good" and "evil," determined by the government and the dominant values within the state.

Within this context, a clear need arises to discuss the so-called "new ethics," one which is removed from the schematic thinking on good and evil, ingrained through stereotypes. In this regard, an important role could be played by "situational ethics," which rejects any moral norms, appealing instead to conscience and moral awareness, postulating the necessity of individual responsibility for moral decisions taken within a particular context. It would also seem important to also consider the assumptions behind the "independent ethics" ("ethics of care"), proposed by T. Kotarbiński (Kotarbiński, 1970: 94). This ethics is "free" of any particular world-view. Therefore, its foundations cannot "collapse" because of a crisis of faith. This is a highly universal ethics, nearly intuitive. It is based on the actions of a "good man," a "reliable guardian" concerned with the fate of others, independently of "stale" moral norms. It appeals to the conscience and moral consciousness of each individual, who should take decisions of a moral nature under their own responsibility.

It would seem that all modern ethical considerations must be linked to the theoretical determinations of the other domains within philosophy, both epistemology and metaphysics. They should also take into account "new" proposals, relating not only to general ethics but also to that of virtue and role models, the standards for which have been defined on the basis of normative ethics. These rules can at times "collide" with the research results of descriptive ethicists. It therefore becomes necessary to take into account the assumptions behind applied and situational ethics, adapted for the conditions of modernity.

TRADITIONAL DOMAINS OF ETHICAL CONSIDERATIONS

The term "ethics" was introduced by Aristotle in antiquity to define one part of his "practical philosophy." Ethical reflections became part of the Socratic dialogues. Socrates compared his role in discussions of morality to that of a midwife, helping to "extract" true knowledge of good and evil, stuck between layers of apparent knowledge and falsehood, from his interlocutor. The term itself comes from the Greek *ethikos* (relating to morals). Today, it describes the philosophical discipline dealing with morality and moral systems. It is understood as the systematisation of rules and norms pertaining to morality as practised, regulating the behaviour within a given community. At times, this term is also understood as a new project for such regulations, inspired by a specific philosophical direction.

Ethicists are concerned with the analysis of moral concepts. They determine what people consider good, evil, legitimate, illegitimate, just or unjust. They define the basis for differentiating between these categories. The foundation of any ethical considerations is therefore

Ethics and the Challenges of the Contemporary World 7

axiology, which is the study of values of all kinds, in particular those relating to modes of existence and the justification for the enforcement of supra-individual first-order values, which are sometimes nearly entirely elusive.

Social pluralism implies a multiplicity of beliefs, religions, ways of living, subcultures and fashions; various ways of understanding what is good and what is evil; what is beautiful or ugly; what should be practised and that which should not. Individual moral systems are obviously culturally-determined, while in democracies, the dominant morality is based on the fundamental ethical values developed by European culture. It undoubtedly remains influenced by American, or Anglo-Saxon culture in general. Independently of shared cultural determinants, even those living within a specific cultural sphere (such as Europe) show divergence within their moral judgements on numerous controversial topics (e.g., abortion, euthanasia, attitudes regarding the death penalty or refugees etc.).

Conflicts regarding values intensify when two widely different, yet culturally-linked outlooks collide: the secular, linked to the ideals of liberalism, and represented by utilitarianism, consequentialism or naturalistic environmental ethics, and the religious, grounded in the influences of Christian personalism (Kopciuch, Siwiec, 2014: 13-48, 97, 347; Saja, 2015). Secularism is undoubtedly one of the pillars of Western humanism. According to R. Braidotti, an instinctive aversion to churches and religion lies at its basis (Braidotti, 2014: 92).

We could note that from the moment of inception of the utilitarian "moral arithmetic" (a calculus of the profits and losses deriving from moral choices), this manner of thinking has been at odds with the absolute, autotelic values of Catholicism. The concept of quality of life conflicts markedly with that of its sacredness and absolute inviolability (Chańska, 2015: 13-66).

CLASSIFICATION OF ETHICS WITHIN THE MODERN PHILOSOPHICAL DISCOURSE

Within ethics we can denote "general" and "special ethics." As a philosophical domain, ethics is further divided into: "descriptive ethics," "normative ethics," "situational ethics" and "applied ethics." Ever more often, among the domains of ethics, we find "global ethics," "environmental ethics" (or "ecological") and "bioethics." Within this context, we should note the meaning of "ethical naturalism" (Makowski, 2012: 120-127). We can note that along with the popularity of ecological awareness, we can see the rise of "consumer ethics," undoubtedly associated with the concept of sustainable development (e.g., the Slow Food or Fair Trade movements). Furthermore, among universal ethics, we can also note the emergence of "informational ethics." It should be noted that in the current "information age," in which the world is defined mostly by information and the technologies used to process it, this is becoming particularly important. The concept of information is gradually increasing its scope of meaning. From a term relating to communications, it is expanding into a biological category. Today, cybernetic systems transmitting information do not need to be either living or conscious (Internet of Things). Information which crosses the boundaries of cybernetics is currently seen as a philosophical category. Its application to issues relating to the nature of existence, cognition and values offers news ways of understanding "old" problems. It is implicated in the creation of the cybernetic concept of man as an "autonomous system." Let us note that autonomous cybernetic systems (i.e., "software agents," "electronic agents," "robots") mimic human beings. They are escaping the control of programmers ever more often, becoming similar to independent beings (Kilchowski, 2014: 149; Bińczyk, 2012: 259; Braidotti, 2014: 239-247). The following question remains open: when will artificial intelligence start to sin and what could be the consequences form a global ethical perspective? The manner of defining human subjectivity becomes a moral and legal problem. This is not limited to autonomous robots. For instance, how do we define the "creatures" which result from the practice of *BioArt*? What is the nature of the being created as the result of the work of someone like Eduardo Kac, who embedded his own, human DNA into a petunia plant: a "plantimal"? And if so, then what legal protections should it enjoy?

The doubts noted above, relating to the general perspectives of ethics, are formulated in relation to the problems arising from practical ethics, to which both applied and situational ethics belong. In its most general form, practical ethics consists in implementing the results of theoretical research into real, everyday life. It should be noted that it is precisely the wisdom "embodied" in the traditions of a given social group (community) which determines its course of action. It allows man to confront the problems facing him, constituting the justification and starting point for the decisions he makes. The assumptions of general ethics, applied to a given situation, are one such point. Which is why it becomes necessary to familiarise ourselves with them.

THE ROLE OF GENERAL ETHICS IN SOCIAL LIFE

General ethics deals with the issues concerning what constitutes the good, duty, conscience, responsibility and what should be the goal of human action. From the earliest times, philosophers have attempted to determine how to live a good and pleasant life which brings happiness (both as individuals and as part of society). Numerous ethical theories have been, and continue to be, devised so as to provide "advice" on how to lead a satisfying life, both from a personal and global perspective. These are the proposals of what is called "normative ethics." They define standard models of how to act so that a given behaviour can be perceived as "good," from the point of view of the dominant morality. Such "recipes" have been proposed by philosophers since antiquity, contained in concepts such as Aristotle's "golden mean," Plato's "cavern," Epicurus' "garden of happiness," the "dog-like life" of the Cynics or the imprecations of the Stoics to disregard that over which we have no control. In modern times, these "recipes" appear as part of Christian ethics and in many other forms: Kantian ethics, liberalism, contractualism, utilitiarianism, existentialism or post-modernism. It is worth noting that the fundamental rules of various ethical theories, present and past, are absorbed during the process of socialisation, becoming an integral part of individual moral systems.

And although single-factor proposals, unconditionally embodied within public life often result in nefarious consequences (e.g., Plato's ideals became the justification for the functioning of totalitarian systems), yet certain elements of various concepts can play the part of "moral signposts," within both individual and collective life. They allow to navigate the shifting "ethical grounds," in particular within the context of globalisation (and its implied convergence and divergence of values) and technological progress (and its consequences in terms of opportunities, challenges and dangers).

Within general ethics which, as previously mentioned, determines normative models of behaviour, we distinguish what is called "virtue ethics and role models." It is based on perfectionism and, apart from norms and principles, also propagates virtues and specific behaviour patterns which should be imitated. It posits that man shall strive to achieve "higher" goals. Its postulate is the production of the "morally excellent man," through the development of his personal virtues and the eradication of his defects. Often, this entails ethical rigorism. According to this view, excellence constitutes the highest moral good, which both individuals and groups should strive to achieve. Most probably without full justification, it is accepted that what is good and evil can be defined once and for all.

We should not forget that the world of values is a complicated one. There are both "positive" values (pluses) and "negative" values

Ethics and the Challenges of the Contemporary World 11

(minuses), while alongside virtue ethics and role models, there exists also a "bandit morality" (that of the thief). The ambiguity of the criteria defining "good and "evil" implies that, depending on the civilisational level and local conditions (e.g., national, professional or familial), the category of moral justness can be understood differently. In the individual moral systems of each person, there exist elements of both virtue ethics role models and the bandit morality. The latter appear as the moral acceptance of behaviours generally considered unethical (e.g., infidelity). In everyday life, people "oscillate" somewhere between good and evil, devising justifications for acts not fully in compliance with accepted morality. For example, this is particularly visible in post-socialist countries of Central and Eastern Europe as the particular inheritance of socialism and Christianity life (Kołakowski, 2014; Tischner, 2005). Lies, corruption and nepotism were the order of the day. These types of unethical behaviours found their legitimisation in the lack of acceptance of the imposed, undemocratic system. They were the expression of a sociological division between: "civil society" (which had just started to form) and the "authorities" (which had not yet achieved bottom-up acceptance). They were justified by a pragmatic approach towards life. Which makes the role of adequate education on ethics all the more important in the post-socialist European countries.

THE NATURE OF APPLIED ETHICS WITHIN THE CONTEXT OF PROFESSIONAL DEONTOLOGY

Education concerning ethics should insist in particular on the tenets of "special ethics." It belongs to a field within normative ethics which underlines the necessity for the strict and absolute respect of ethical rules, as expressed within various ethical codes devised for people fulfilling specific social roles.

The basis for discipline-specific ethics is Kantian ethics, according to which ethical acts must be in accordance with moral law (indicated by the categorical imperative) as well as resulting from a feeling of duty. A particular role is played by the assumption of ethical formalism and rigorism. Above all, emphasis is placed on the necessity of actions conforming with externally applicable norms. The internal feelings of the acting entity become a secondary issue. The most important aspect is the "ethics of responsibility." It requires that people accomplish the tasks required of them and identify with the community in which they live.

It should be noted that the deontological approach to ethics contains many pitfalls. They are most apparent when looking through the prism of religious deontology which implies the necessity of fulfilling obligations which are accepted as the indisputable dogmas of faith. On the other hand, the proper and rational establishment and respect of deontological rules (e.g., in professions of public trust) appears indispensable today.

It is precisely special ethics which form the basis for the determination of the principles of moral action, in relation to the most important situations and categories of human activity. Professional deontology occupies a particularly important place in this, specifying the set of moral norms which indicate how representatives of a specific profession should act.

Professional ethics, also called "professional deontology," grew from the notion of "moral duty" (moral obligation). Its standards are defined in various sets of deontological norms. The most formalised ones are undoubtedly professional codes of ethics. They are established (based on a statutory mandate) for a specific profession, part of the "professions of public trust" or "liberal professions." As a matter of doctrine, it is accepted that these types of professions are entrusted with a particular mission, one which includes the need of making professional decisions dealing with the most fundamental questions in relation to human existence (life, health, property or freedom). These

Ethics and the Challenges of the Contemporary World 13

doctrinal determinations imply that those representing the professions endowed with the public trust should act *pro bono publico* (for the public good). This means that in the event of a conflict between the public interest and the personal interest of the person representing the profession, the good of the client and the public takes precedence (over the personal good).

The specificity of professions of public trust implies the principles of loyalty and confidentiality. Those representing professions of public trust are often entrusted with very private, intimate, or sensitive information. Hence why professional secrecy plays such an important role here. The "moral reputation" of representatives of a given profession is defined by "ethical standards," oaths of office (vows) and unwritten rules (e.g., fair play, best practises, good moral standing etc.). In its modern form, professionalism implies not only having the required knowledge and skills, but also a "high" level of ethical competence.

Although doctrinal considerations often argue against the need of creating professional codes of ethics, professional deontologist would appear to be necessary. Irrespective of what some describe as merely a "façade," fulfilling an "ornamental" role, or a "manicure" on a clenched fist, in any case ready to strike its opponent. Yet these attempts to discredit the necessity of creating professional codes of conduct, by underlining that an honest man will remain honest, both at home and at work, and so a code is spurious, ultimately fail to convince.

It is undeniably correct that specially-developed codes of ethics do not significantly raise the morals of specific professions. In practice, we see that despite defined norms, some professions are clearly more susceptible to immoral and deviant behaviour than others (e.g., Tokarczyk, 2007). This is a vital argument in this discussion, which could testify to the lack of necessity of deontological norms. It would seem however that written standards of morality play a largely positive role by providing "moral signposts" for behaviour, teaching responsibility and helping to resolve the conflicts which can appear within specific professions.

However, it is often the case that general ethics is insufficient and, under particular circumstances, may even be in contradiction with special ethics. Let us consider the ethics of medicine. The main deontological principles within this profession are: *primum non nocere* and *salus aegroti suprema lex*. A doctor has an unconditional duty to save a life which is in danger. Let us imagine how we would act as "normal" people (without medical training), if we found ourselves in a situation in which we must rescue the victims of an accident. Let us suppose one is a drunken driver, and the other a small child. The normal human reaction would be to attempt to save the child first. Doctors, however, must act according to the deontological rules governing their profession. Their duty is to help the person whose life is most at risk (even if this were to be the drunken driver). Let us further note that certain characteristics, desirable from the point of view of general ethics, can be undesirable within the context of professional codes of ethics (e.g., excessive empathy and sensitivity to human suffering could prevent a judge from handing down objective rulings). General and special ethics are thereby clearly distinct. However, each obviously considers human dignity as a fundamental value. It is worth noting that the norms of general ethics can apply to situations which are not defined by special ethics.

DISSONANCE BETWEEN NORMATIVE AND DESCRIPTIVE ETHICS

A certain dissonance is perceptible between the normative sphere (indicating the expected standards of behaviour) and the descriptive sphere (which shows "things as they are"). The determinations made by descriptive ethics often conflict brutally with the sphere of being.

Ethics and the Challenges of the Contemporary World 15

Descriptive ethics is also known as "ethology" (from the Greek *ethos* – character). It deals with the analysis of morality as a social phenomenon. It is used as a basis for describing existing morality. This is done either from a historical or a modern perspective. In the first case, it attempts to determine what was considered good, and what evil, in a specific era. The second examines the morality of a specific social group (e.g., a profession) at a given time and place.

The published results of sociological research are quite alarming (Komunikat Centrum Badania Opinii Społecznej w Polsce, BS/164/2013: 8). They indicate that some of the most demoralised groups of professionals are those active in domains relating to politics, administration, law, business and medicine. This should come as no surprise, since it has been common knowledge for centuries that the intersection between the spheres of politics, government and money is conducive to corruption, nepotism and the abuse of influence and decision-making for private gain. The results obtained indicate that those supposedly forming the "moral elite" are, in fact, its "moral plebs" (Tokarczyk, 2007: 13). Perhaps this is due to an improper understanding of the nature of professionalism.

Let us note that in many post-communist countries, for a long time, the main demands made of those working in professions of public trust (e.g., politicians or lawyers) were competence and effectiveness. Unethical private behaviours by public servants were condoned in an untypical manner. It sufficed that they performed their professional duties adequately. There is a famous anecdote concerning a well-known Marxist ethicist during the 1980s. His impetuous temper, fondness for drink and proclivity for young women were widely known in academic circles. His students accused him, in his role as a university lecturer, of "immoral behaviour" which, they noted, was "unseemly for a professional." The ethicist responded curtly to these accusations: "an ornithologist need not know how to fly" and "a signpost does not head in the direction it shows." In the 21st century, these types of explanations would surely not find universal acceptance. Today, those

16 *Anetta Breczko and Agata Breczko*

filling certain social roles are required to possess not only the required expertise, but also the requisite moral competence, based on the assumptions of virtue ethics and role models. This pertains not only to the professional sphere, but also to private life (Tokarczyk, 2007: 49-51).

THE PLACE OF APPLIED ETHICS AND SITUATIONAL ETHICS WITHIN CONTEMPORARY PHILOSOPHICAL CONSIDERATIONS

The considerations of applied ethics are used as a basis determining the "moral condition" of a given social group through practical research. Ethicists ask specific questions concerning hypothetical moral behaviours to "measure" the defining morality of a given environment. The answers of the respondents will not always correspond to their "actual morality." However, their analysis allows to determine certain standards in relation to "expected" behaviour. The objects of applied ethics studies are ethical dilemmas, appearing both in everyday life and as "hard cases"), which are common in judicial proceedings. In general, their specificity is the lack of a correct answer, which would help resolve the collision of values. The respondent is faced with a moral choice consisting of the "lesser evil." Although none of the choices can be "good," it is however necessary to make a specific moral decision. This takes place in comfortable conditions, far removed from those which might appear in real contexts in everyday life.

Ethicists ask numerous questions, using examples which have become classics, such as the "lifeboat dilemma," "trolley problem" or "bridge dilemma" ("viaduct"). The first deals with providing an answer to the following hypothetical situation: you must decide whether you would throw someone overboard, if you knew there was no other possibility. Otherwise, the lifeboat sinks. You must choose between

Ethics and the Challenges of the Contemporary World   17

sacrificing one person's life, so that the others make it, or placing your trust in "divine providence," without attempting to save anyone. The lifeboat contains several people, including a pregnant woman, a small child and an old man. From the perspective of Christian ethics, in general, the answer is that the "sacrifice" of the pregnant woman is absolutely unacceptable. Because she carries another life. The possibility of throwing the child overboard is also excluded, due to the great potential of its future existence. Within the European cultural sphere, the most common answer is that the life of the old man is the "price" for saving the others. Since its "quality" could only decline. However, when trying to use the utilitarian calculus of profits and losses in practice, the possibility that the child could grow up to be a war criminal (such as Stalin or Hitler) or that the old man could still bring many benefits to society (e.g., by inventing a drug for an incurable disease or creating an outstanding work of art) is often forgotten. On the other hand, the Christian personalism implies that the "valuation" of any life is forbidden. Which is why the only legitimate solution to solving this dilemma would be to trust in "divine providence." The fact that an attempt is nevertheless made to use "moral arithmetic" could indicate that it is in fact more intuitive and, maybe, "more human" than religious assumptions.

The previously mentioned dilemmas of the "trolley" and the "bridge" have led to the emergence of a micro-specialisation, jokingly called "trolleyology" (Cathcart, 2014: 9). The "trolley problem" was introduced by the British philosopher P. Foot in 1967. It proposes a hypothetical situation in which a runaway trolley is speeding down the railway tracks. The driver sees five people on the tracks. He can remain on the main track and kill them all (for some reason they cannot move). Or he can switch to a side track, killing only one person. Should the driver exit the main track and kill one person instead of five? How should an observer act? Should the observer let fate play itself out? Or activate the switch and cause the death of one person, saving five others? Let us further imagine the situation devised by J. Thomson. A person on the railway bridge can see the impending catastrophe. The runaway trolley is arriving, with five people tied to the track facing certain death if he fails to act. There is a fat man standing next to him: if he falls on the track, his bulk would stop the trolley. Should he push him over the bridge to save the other five? (Cathcart, 2014: 10-12).

When faced with such a situation, most of us would probably resort to using the utilitarian calculus. Few consider that according to Christian dogma, no human life can have any valuation and so "fate" should be accepted; there is however another way of combining utilitarianism and religion in this situation. After all, it is possible to sacrifice one's own life to save the others. The instinct of self-preservation or, perhaps, human egoism, usually suggests another choice.

Let us use another example to demonstrate the importance of "moral convictions" ("moral sense"), which cannot be verified rationally. T. Cathcart's book describes the fictional case of a trauma surgeon summoned to the accident and emergency unit of a local clinic. There was an accident on the motorway. Several of the injured have arrived. A doctor has checked on them and determined two require kidney transplants; a third a heart; the fourth a liver transplant, and the fifth a lung. The surgeon is worried that he will be unable to find donor organs quickly enough when he notices that another, thirty-something man has arrived for observation, without any serious injuries. And so he decides to transplant the man's organs into the other five patients, saving their lives in the process (Cathcart, 2014: 37). This type of rationalisation would surely not be accepted socially.

Let us move on to another problem. Does moral character exist? Are virtue ethics and roles models still relevant? This ethics is considered one of the most important ethical concepts. It posits the necessity of working on one's character, consolidating its relevant characteristics and dispositions (ethical virtues), in the belief that the quality of human acts depends upon the moral condition of those who perform them. This approach has generated numerous publications,

Ethics and the Challenges of the Contemporary World 19

offering relatively consistent ethical concepts proposed by philosophers such as: A. MacIntyre, M. Nussbaum, M. Slote, N. Sherman, J. Annas, R. Audi, R. Hurshouse, Ch. Santon, R. Adams (Szutta, 2013: 65). Many of them relate to Aristotelian virtue ethics, which is a constant point of reference within contemporary debate on character ethics. It is hard to discuss social or political ethics today without referring to civic virtues (e.g., caring, thoughtfulness, honesty or trustworthiness). In fact, professional deontology is based on these virtues.

We should also note that today, the assumptions behind virtue ethics and role models are subjected to a strong situational critique. Numerous experiments are carried out which indicate that the main influences on human action are real situations.

Research carried out by social psychologists has contributed to the popularity of situational ideas. One of the best-known experiments was conducted by S. Milgram in 1963 (Milgram, 2008). Of equal importance was the research carried out by P. Zimbardo (Zimbardo, 2010).

The Milgram experiment consisted in the participants being assigned roles as "teachers" and "learners," with the latter pressured to "obey authority." While the official goal of the experiment was to study the influence of violence on memorisation processes, it turned out that within it, over 60% of the subjects intentionally administered electrical shocks (between 15-450 Volts) to an innocent person, despite increasing objections on their part, until all signs of life had ceased. The subjects were in no way forced to carry out these acts, there were no penalties for stopping the experiment early and neither were they in a position of subordination to the experimenters. They were merely informed that the experiment should continue. The authority of the experimenter was enough to push them to perform acts which were difficult to accept (Szutta 2013, p. 68). Half a century later, the experiment was repeated by Polish social psychologists at the SWPS University in Wrocław. Nearly 70% of the selected "teachers" applied the strongest possible shock (450 V) to their victims (Ulanowski, 2017: 16).

The results of the experiment devised by P. Zimbardo at Stanford were equally worrying. The participants who qualified were all in good mental health, intelligent, mature and balanced. They were randomly placed in two groups: "prisoners" and "guards." The basement of the university was transformed to simulate a high-security prison. The experiment was stopped after six days, after the participants had identified too intensely with their roles. Incidents of verbal and physical abuse had erupted. The subjects had been completely "sucked into" the situation, while those enjoying better conditions ("guards") acted with a high level of cruelty, as if to get "revenge upfront" for the harm they themselves would be subjected to by the current "prisoners" when the roles would be reversed (Szutta, 2013: 68).

When analysing the above experiments, J. M. Doris appears to question the validity of the belief in a fixed moral character, which can be formed through proper education and by internalising the standards of virtue ethics and role models. He draws attention to the differing contexts of human behaviour, which influence it and which depend on the social role which is performed, authority, group and even factors such as mood or haste (Doris, 2002: 32-35). He adds that the explanation of actions by the character type of the person who carries it out is present only in Western culture, which does not allow to be free from the attribution of fixed traits of character to people. Eastern culture on the other hand seems to be dominated by a situational manner of explaining moral decisions (Doris, 2002: 105-106).

Although arguably, the situationists who claim that such an ethics allows to better understand the scale of barbarity present around the world (the Shoah, Rwandan genocide etc.), are also correct. It is easier to build a future by explaining such terrible events by a certain specific situation, than by the moral character of their perpetrators. We should not generalise by supposing that all the people implicated in such atrocities were simply "evil." In part, they were themselves the "victims" of the situation, moral chance and a shared tragic fate.

CONCLUSION

Should we therefore completely reject the assumptions of virtue ethics and role models? This does not appear to be justified. Such an ethics, supplemented with the inclusion of the situationist approach, remains necessary. The shaping of specific moral attitudes and dispositions is deeply rooted within European culture. It determines the manner of human behaviour, contributing to an increase in the responsibility for individual choices. Virtue ethics and role models are of vital importance to the desired building of a "moral reputation" for those representing professions of public trust. Without indicating the "ethical virtues" to which they should aspire, it would prove impossible to construct professional deontologist. A proper ethical education should also serve to adequately shape emotions and motivations by indicating specific models of action. Autonomous man, as a moral entity, guided by his inner morality (implied by cultural conditions), does not allow the situation to lead him astray, but tries to prevail over it by selecting the most appropriate solution from the point of view of an accepted criterion of "good."

REFERENCES

Agamben, G. (2008). *Homo sacer. Suwerenna władza i nagie życie* [*Homo sacer. Sovereign Power and Bare Life*]. Warszawa: Wydawnictwo Prószyński i S-ka Spółka Akcyjna.

22 *Anetta Breczko and Agata Breczko*

Amsterdamski, S. (1987), *Tertium non datur. In Obecność – Leszkowi Kołakowskiemu w 60 rocznicę urodzin [Tertium non datur. In Presence - Leszek Kołakowski on the 60th birthday]*. London.

Bauman, Z. (1995). *A jeśli etyki zabraknie. Kultura współczesna. Teoria. Interpretacje. Krytyka [And if ethics run out. Contemporary culture. Theory. Interpretations. Criticism]*. No. 1-2, 147-159.

Bauman, Z. (1994). *Dwa szkice o moralności ponowoczesnej [Two sketches on postmodern morality]*. Warszawa: Instytut Kultury.

Bińczyk, E. (2012). *Technonauka w społeczeństwie ryzyka. Filozofia wobec niepożądanych następstw praktycznego rozwoju nauki [Technolish in a risk society. Philosophy towards the undesirable consequences of the practical development of science]*. Toruń: Wydawnictwo Naukowe UMK.

Braidotti, R. (2014). *Po człowieku [The Posthuman]*. Warszawa: Państwowe Wydawnictwo Naukowe.

Cathcart, T. (2014). Dylemat wagonika. Czy zrzuciłbyś grubego faceta z kładki? Zagadka filozoficzna. Warszawa: *Państwowe Wydawnictwo Naukowe.* [The Trolley Problem, or Would You Throw the Fat Guy Off the Bridge?: *A Philosophical Conundrum*].

Chamayou, G. (2012). *Podłe ciała. Eksperymenty na ludziach w XVIII i XIX wieku. Gdańsk: Słowo/obraz/terytoria. [Vile Bodies: Experimenting on Human Beings in the 18th and 19th Centuries]*.

Dawkins, R. (2014). Kapłan diabła. *Opowieści o nadziei, kłamstwie, nauce i miłości. Gliwice: Wydawnictwo Helion.* [A *Devil's Chaplain: Reflections of Hope, Lies, Science, and Love*].

Dawkins, R. (2007). *Bóg urojony [The God Delusion]*. Warszawa: Wydawnictwo CiS..

DeGrazia, D. (2014). *Prawa zwierząt.* Kraków: Zakład Wydawniczy Nomos. [*Animal Rights: A Very Short Introduction*].

Doris, J. M. (2002). *Lack of Character*. Cambridge: Cambridge University Press.

Ethics and the Challenges of the Contemporary World 23

Eilstein, H. (1994). *"Homo sapiens i wartości". Eseje.* ["Homo sapiens and values". Essays]. Warszawa: Państwowe Wydawnictwo Naukowe.

Harrington, K. (1997). *Historia kar i tortur* [*History of Punishment and Torture*]. Ciemna strona wymiaru sprawiedliwości. Warszawa: Elipsa.

Kilchowski, M. (2014). *Narodziny cyborgizacji* [*The birth of cyborgization*]. Nowa eugenika, transhumanizm i zmierzch edukacji. Poznań: Wydawnictwo Naukowe UAM.

Kołakowski, L. (2014). *Niepewność epoki demokracji* [*Uncertainty of the age of democracy*]. Kraków: Wydawnictwo Znak.

Kołakowski, L. (2000). *Kultura i fetysze. Zbiór rozpraw* [*Culture and fetishes. Collection of hearings*]. Warszawa: Państwowe Wydawnictwo Naukowe.

Kotarbiński, T. (1980). *Studia z zakresu filozofii etyki i nauk społecznych* [*Studies in the philosophy of ethics and social sciences*]. Wrocław: Zakład Narodowy im. Ossolińskich.

Makowski, P. (2012). *Po metafizyce. Dobro i powinność w etykach naturalistycznych* [*After metaphysics. Good and duty in naturalistic ethics*]. Kraków: Towarzystwo Autorów i wydawców Prac Naukowych Universitas.

Milgram, S. (2008). *Posłuszeństwo wobec autorytetu* [*Obedience to Authority*]. Kraków: Państwowe Wydawnictwo Naukowe.

Probucka, D. (2013). *Filozoficzne podstawy idei praw zwierząt* [*The philosophical foundations of the idea of animal rights*]. Kraków: Towarzystwo Autorów i Wydawców Prac Naukowych Universitas.

Putnam, H. (2004). *Ethics without Ontology*. Cambridge: Harvard University Press.

Saja, K. (2015). *Etyka normatywna. Między konsekwencjonalizmem a deontologią* [*Normative ethics. Between consequentialism and deontology*]. Kraków: Towarzystwo Autorów i wydawców Prac Naukowych Universitas.

Schmidt-Salomon, M. (2013). *Poza dobrem i złem* [*Beyond Good and Evil*]. Słupsk: Wydawnictwo Dobra Literatura.

Sykuna, S. (2009), Filozofia prawa a multikulturalizm – studium przypadku. In D. Bunikowski, K. Dobrzeniecki, (Eds.), *Pluralizm prawny, tradycja, transformacje, wyzwania* [Philosophy of law and multiculturalism - a case study. In D. Bunikowski, K. Dobrzeniecki, (Eds.), *Legal pluralism, tradition, transformations, challenges*] (pp. 189-204). Toruń. Poland: Interdyscyplinarne Koło Naukowe Doktorantów UMK.

Szutta N. (2013). *Czy istnieje charakter moralny? Dyskusja z Johna Dorisa sytuacjonistyczną krytyką etyki cnót* [*Is there a moral character? A discussion of John Doris with a situationist critique of the ethics of virtues*]. Etyka No. 46, pp. 66-87.

Tischner, J. (2005). *Etyka solidarności oraz homo sovieticus* [*Ethics of solidarity and homo sovieticus*], Kraków: Wydawnictwo Znak.

Tokarczyk, R. (2007), *Etyka prawnicza* [*Legal ethics*], Warszawa: Wydawnictwo Prawnicze LexisNexis.

Traverso, E. (2003). *The Origins of Nazi Violence*, New York: The New Press.

Ulanowski, T. (2017). Polacy elektryzująco posłuszni [*Poles electrifyingly obey*]. *Gazeta Wyborcza,* 1.03.2017, 16-17.

Zarosa, U. (2016). *Status moralny zwierząt* [*Moral status of animals*]. Warszawa: Państwowe Wydawnictwo Naukowe.

Zimbardo P. (2010). *Efekt Lucyfera. Dlaczego dobrzy ludzie czynią zło?* [*The Lucifer Effect: Understanding How Good People Turn Evil*] Warszawa: Państwowe Wydawnictwo Naukowe.

In: Ethics
Editor: Miles Ventura

ISBN: 978-1-53613-533-6
© 2018 Nova Science Publishers, Inc.

Chapter 2

MONISM, DUALISM, AND SUPERVENIENCE: A DEBATE ON DISTRIBUTIVE JUSTICE

Benedict S. B. Chan[*]
Department of Religion and Philosophy,
Hong Kong Baptist University, Hong Kong, China

ABSTRACT

What is the relationship between politics and morality? In this chapter, I discuss Nagel's dualism and Murphy's monism in depth. Both of them limit their discussions to distributive justice, but they admit that their views can apply to a more general discussion of the relationship between politics and morality. On one hand, Nagel argues that distributive justice can only be assured by nation-states because only states have *associative responsibility*; associative responsibility does not apply to any particular individual. On the other hand, Murphy argues that we should assure justice by both institutions and individuals, and only monism could explain why a person should act to assure justice in non-ideal situations. Both arguments have strengths and weaknesses. Nagel tells us how important sovereignty is, and Murphy tells us how important

---

[*] Corresponding Author Email: benedictchan@hkbu.edu.hk.

it is to assure justice. Nevertheless, Nagel fails to explain why individuals are not required to assure justice, and Murphy fails to explain how principles of justice can apply to individuals. The most important problem is that they do not have the same standard to evaluate and justify both positions. Although both of them have their own reasons to support their own view, it is unclear how they can refute the opposite side. I suggest that supervenience is the key to solve this problem. I use supervenience as a standard to evaluate arguments from both sides, and then argue that a supervenience relationship between politics and morality would be the third and better position than both dualism and monism.

Keywords: politics, morality, justice, dualism, monism, supervenience

INTRODUCTION

What is the relationship between politics and morality? Many philosophers have tried to answer this question, and in this chapter, I focus on two of them: dualism from Nagel (2005) and monism from Murphy (1998). Their ideas are particularly related to distributive justice. I evaluate their arguments in depth and then I discuss my argument. My suggestion is that we should use supervenience as a standard to evaluate the arguments of Nagel and Murphy, and I also argue that a supervenience relationship between politics and morality is a better position than both dualism and monism. The structure of this chapter is as follows: I first discuss Nagel's dualism and Murphy's monism, especially their strengths and weaknesses, and then I place supervenience into the debate between dualism and monism and argue for my own position.

NAGEL'S DUALISM

Murphy describes dualism as "the two practical problems of institutional design and personal conduct require, at the fundamental level, two different kinds of practical principle" (Murphy, 1998, pp. 253–54). For example, Murphy categorizes Rawls as a dualist. Rawls' general idea is that justice is the first virtue of social institutions, and "[t]he principles of justice for institutions must not be confused with the principles which apply to individuals and their actions in particular circumstances. These two kinds of principles apply to different subjects and must be discussed separately" (Rawls, 1999, p. 47). Rawls thinks that his principles of justice apply only to the political institutions of a society but do not apply to any particular individual (pp. 24–25).

Nagel agrees with Rawls and so he also considers himself a dualist. He thinks that it is the nature of sovereign states that creates the special demands for distributive justice. Principles of distributive justice are normative principles for the distribution of property; they set up some constraints on how property can be distributed justly. Nagel (2005) thinks that principles of distributive justice should only be designed specifically to nation-states. He writes:

> Sovereign states are not merely instruments for realizing the pre-institutional value of justice among human beings. Instead, their existence is precisely what gives the value of justice its application . . . an institutional relation which must then be evaluated by the special standards of fairness and equality that fill out the content of justice (p. 120).

> [Rawls'] two principles of justice are designed to regulate neither the personal conduct of individuals living in a just society, nor the governance of private associations, nor the international relations of

societies to one another, but only the basic structure of separate nation-states. (p. 123)[1]

In general, Nagel's main argument is that distributive justice depends on *associative responsibility*, which is only created by specific relations within a state. He thinks that distributive justice is a right that people only have when they join together in a political society under strong centralized control. Principles of justice are subject to the system of collective authority only; these principles do not apply to the action of each individual citizen.

Nagel's argument has two important points. The first is about the coercively imposed power of a state. Nagel argues that justice should only apply to people who join in a strong and coercively imposed political institution because justice can only be assured through laws and centralized authority. He thinks that citizens of a state are putative joint authors of the coercively imposed system who are also subjected to its norm. Nagel's idea comes from Hobbes' idea that there can be no justice if there is no government. According to Hobbes, people cannot assure justice by themselves; sovereignty is required to assure justice in a society because everyone is self-interested, and so a single force is required to assure justice or any collective self-interest (Hobbes, 1651, Chapter 13). People may not agree with Hobbes that the foundation of justice is collective self-interest. Nevertheless, regarding what moral motivations individuals have for justice, sovereignty is required to confer stability on political institutions because justice can only be assured through laws and centralized authority. The whole idea implies

---

[1] More precisely, Nagel argues something more than dualism, which can be called "the multi-layered conception of morality." He thinks that normative principles for nation-states should neither apply to individuals nor global institutions (this is also why he thinks that there is no global distributive justice). Nevertheless, he agrees with other dualists that normative principles for politics should be distinct from normative principles for individuals, and his arguments against global justice do not affect the discussion here. Therefore, I think that his idea about nation-states' associative responsibility can still be considered as a significant argument to support dualism.

Monism, Dualism, and Supervenience 29

that a government with coercively imposed power is special and necessary to assure justice (Nagel, 2005, pp. 115–117).

Another point in Nagel's (2005) argument is that citizens join their own state involuntarily. He writes: "A sovereign state is not just a cooperative enterprise for mutual advantage. The societal rules determining its basic structure are coercively imposed: it is not a voluntary association" (p. 128). Nagel thinks that justice is a rise in exclusive obligation with a broad associative range, and so justice depends on the contingency of involuntary rather than voluntary association. He also thinks that a sovereign state is obviously not a voluntary association. Since joining a state is usually involuntary, it should meet a higher standard than voluntary combinations, which are governed by standards of equality.

Coercion and involuntariness assure that states have special *authorities* and special *responsibilities* to their citizens. It is in the nature of sovereign states to create special demands for justice; thus, the principles of justice are designed specifically for them. Those principles of justice are subject to the system of collective authority and justification as a whole only; they are not subject to any particular citizen. Citizens, of course, have responsibilities to their states as well. For example, citizens should try their best to assure that their governments consider and decide public policies based on the principles of justice. However, the individual actions of each citizen do not need to follow the principles of justice. Indeed, the principles of justice are not designed according to any individual moral rule, and so it is not applicable to any individual's choice and action (Nagel, 2005, p. 123). In summary, Nagel agrees with Rawls that individuals are free to pursue their own personal ends, and the principles of justice apply only to the society as a whole. In other words, individuals are not expected to be governed by these principles of justice.

Murphy's Monism

Murphy (1998) describes monism like this: "Any plausible overall political/moral view must, at the fundamental level, evaluate the justice of institutions with normative principles that apply also to people's choices" (pp. 253–54). He does not think that normative principles for political institutions should be fundamentally different from the principles for individuals. He argues against different versions of dualism in his paper, and his main argument for monism is that only monism can reasonably explain what a person should do to assure justice. He writes:

> It seems to me that any political theory that accepts Rawls's bifurcation of the normative realm into one set of principles for institutions and another for people will yield an implausible account of what people should do in nonideal circumstances. Thus there is a general reason to reject dualism (p. 279).

Murphy notes that the core part of dualism is that there are politically normative principles that do not apply to individuals, and individuals should at most only support and promote just institutions. When individuals can assure justice without political institutions in some situations, there is no reason not to extend the principles of justice to personal conducts. He argues that there are some non-ideal situations that can illustrate his view. Now let me explain his argument in depth.

Dualists hold a view that there should be two sets of normative principles, one set for political institutions and another set for individuals. Dualists think that some moral rules require individuals to assist in the establishment of just institutions, but individuals do not need to act according to the content of the principles of justice. Murphy disagrees with dualists. He argues that if we believe that a society should have distributive justice, then we should assure justice by both institutions and individuals. Distributive justice is about the fairness of

Monism, Dualism, and Supervenience 31

property distribution in a society; if we believe that justice as fairness is a good virtue, and we believe that principles of justice can justify and distribute property reasonably, then there is no reason for us to stand aside and do nothing. He writes:

> If people can do more to promote the aims of justice [,] a view that refuses to extend the principles of justice to personal conduct is prima facie deficient . . . If people have a duty to promote just institutions, why do they lack a duty to promote whatever it is that just institutions are *for*? (pp. 279–280)

Murphy neither thinks that principles of justice should only apply to individuals nor that political institutions have nothing to do to assure justice. He admits that sometimes the most effective way to assure justice is to promote just institutions. He also agrees that a state government that has sovereign power can assure justice effectively, especially in an ideal situation. But this is, at most, a practical reason for individuals to assure justice by political institutions, and it does not grant any *fundamental* normative role to political institutions. It also does not exclude the moral role of individuals to assure justice at all.

Murphy thinks that his idea can be shown clearly in some non-ideal situations. One can imagine many reasons why political institutions cannot assure justice. For example, a country in a civil war may have a government (or governments) that is too weak and does not have enough coercive power. A tyrannical state may have a lot of corrupt government officers, and they are usually the reason for unfair distribution of property. Some may also argue that global institutions (e.g., WTO, IMF) cannot assure justice. Under these circumstances, Murphy argues that there is no reason for us to believe in dualism. He claims that dualism does not require a person to assure justice even if that person could do more to assure justice than to promote or reform the political institutions. Murphy thinks that this is absurd. If billionaires can donate their money directly to hospitals or schools to

32   *Benedict S. B. Chan*

reduce inequality in a society, then it is not necessary for them to use the money to form other political parties or to set up political action committees to assure equality of medicine and education (Murphy, 1998, p. 282). Again, the point here is that politics may not always be the best way to assure justice, especially in a non-ideal situation. Murphy thinks that dualists only want to assure justice through political institutions, while monists can use whatever available means they have to promote justice. Assuring justice through political institutions is, of course, one of the means, but it is never the only option for monists.

In summary, Murphy thinks that justice is a virtue that every society requires, and so we should assure justice by both institutions and individuals. He does not deny that principles of justice can apply to political institutions, but he thinks that these principles can also apply to individuals, provided that individuals can assure justice better than political institutions in some circumstances. Normative principles for political institutions, at the fundamental level, do not have any unique role independent from other normative principles for individuals. Therefore, he thinks that monism is better than dualism because monism allows people to assure justice by both institutions and individuals.

STRENGTHS AND WEAKNESSES

In this section, I first discuss some advantages and disadvantages of Nagel's and Murphy's arguments, and then I argue that both suffer from the same problem. I discuss Nagel's argument first. The most significant idea from Nagel is that sovereignty is very important in the domain of justice. Nagel tries to prove that sovereignty is a necessary condition to assure justice. In other words, Nagel thinks that there can be no justice if there is no sovereign power. Although this position is controversial (Murphy definitely disagrees with it), at least Nagel has

Monism, Dualism, and Supervenience 33

provided an account to explain why sovereignty is so important and effective in assuring justice.

Nevertheless, Nagel fails to explain why normative principles for nation-states are fundamental and independent from normative principles for individuals. It is a big jump from the claim that "sovereignty is important (or even essential) in assuring justice" to the claim that "principles of justice for nation-states are fundamental." Even if sovereignty is such an important factor or even a *necessary* condition for assuring justice, sovereignty is still not a *sufficient* condition for assuring justice. In other words, a state with sovereign power does not guarantee that the distribution of property in the state is just. For example, a tyrannous state may have absolute sovereign power to its citizens, but the distribution of property can be seriously unjust (e.g., all property is controlled by the tyrant). However, the most serious problem is that it is unclear why sovereignty can become a threshold to support the claim that normative principles of political institutions are not related to the normative principles of individuals. Nagel is correct in saying that a sovereign state has coercively imposed power on its citizens, but this does not imply that the normative rules for a sovereign state have no relationship to general ethics. My point here is not that sovereignty definitely cannot be a reason to support dualism. I just simply want to claim that there is no such implication at face value, and the inference from Nagel is not clear. More clarifications are required before one can justify his version of dualism.

The weakness of Nagel's argument is the starting point to discuss the advantage of Murphy's argument. Nagel cannot explain dualism without further clarification, and Murphy would reply that there can be no explanation for dualism. An advantage of Murphy's argument is that he does not need to deny the importance of sovereignty for justice. He can agree that in an ideal situation, the best way to assure justice is to promote political institutions. However, he disagrees that there can be no justice when the situation is non-ideal. His assumption is that justice is good and it is a fundamental moral value; thus, we should assure justice by all means.

However, justice as a fundamental moral value is an assumption that requires further verification. Why is justice so good that we need to assure it by both institutions and individuals? Why is justice not only a problem for political institutions? Dualists, of course, need to provide an answer to the latter question, but Murphy also needs to answer why justice is a fundamental value. Another problem for Murphy is that it is unclear how one can apply the *principles* of justice to individuals. In his paper, the principles of justice he evaluates are from John Rawls, but Rawls' principles are explicitly designed for political institutions. For example, Rawls has a difference principle in his principles of justice, and this difference principle requires that economic inequalities are arranged so that they are to be to the greatest benefit of the least advantaged members of the society (Rawls, 1999, p. 266). It is quite unclear how this can be a normative principle to guide personal conduct. Does it mean that I need to benefit the least advantaged members of my society when I want to buy a car? Murphy owes us an explanation here.

Both dualists and monists have their own motivations to support their positions, and motivations from both sides are reasonable. Dualists want to separate normative principles for politics from individuals because they find that combining them may bring more problems than solutions. For example, on the one hand, dualists may think that it may not be easy—or that it may even be impossible—to apply Rawls' second principle to individual conduct. On the other hand, monists also have a reasonable motivation. Intuitively, if justice or other social values are so good and are required in our society, we should try to assure justice by all reasonable means. So, it is reasonable to wonder why we cannot consider morality as fundamental, and why we need to separate normative principles into two sets.

Both Nagel and Murphy limit their discussions to distributive justice, but they admit that their views can apply to a more general

Monism, Dualism, and Supervenience 35

discussion of the relationship between politics and morality. Although their motivations and reasons are not absurd, it is especially unclear when they use the term *fundamental* to discuss the relationship between politics and morality. On the one hand, when dualists consider political principles as *fundamental*, what they really mean is that political principles are not applicable to individuals. However, it is unclear why political principles need to be fundamental so that they are not applicable to individuals. On the other hand, monists such as Murphy (1998) claim that "[w]hat monism rejects is any defense of such a [political] principle by appeal to a *fundamental* one that does not also apply directly to people's conduct" (p. 254; my italic), and monism does not reject any political principles of a *non-fundamental* kind. Why and how can non-fundamental kinds of political principles apply to individuals? The word "fundamental" and the relationship of politics and morality should be explained further as it is essential to evaluate the arguments between dualism and monism. All we need is a more concrete concept for this discussion. I think this concrete concept is *supervenience*, and this is exactly what I am going to discuss in next section.

SUPERVENIENCE

The concept of supervenience has been well developed in contemporary analytical philosophy. This term probably first appeared in ethics and the philosophy of arts, but later it also became a core concept in metaphysics and the philosophy of mind. Supervenience is a concept about relationships, and philosophers usually use it to discuss the relationship between two sets of properties,[2] A and B. Generally,

---

[2] The meaning of *properties* here is totally different from the word *property* in the discussion of distributive justice. Justice requires us to distribute money and other resources (i.e., property) in a reasonable way. But the concept of properties in the discussion of

supervenience can be considered as a relation of dependency between A and B. If B supervenes on A, then the basic idea is that B depends on A, or A determines B. If A determines B, then it is not possible that A is fixed while B can still vary. A set of B supervenes upon another set of A when two situations cannot differ with respect to B without also differing with respect to A. In other words, there is a covariant relationship from A to B. If two possible situations are indiscernible with respect to A, they are also indiscernible with respect to B. Chalmers (1996) writes the definition like this: "B-properties supervene on A-properties if no two possible situations are identical with respect to their A-properties while differing in their B-properties" (p. 33).

Different philosophers divide the general notion of supervenience into different ways.[3] It turns out that not every detail of supervenience is related to our discussion about Nagel and Murphy, and so I will only discuss the relevant details here. Among those philosophers who have discussed supervenience, Chalmers (1996) has a useful division of supervenience for the debate in this chapter. He divides supervenience further into *conceptual supervenience* and *empirical supervenience*. Empirical supervenience is more useful for the purpose of this chapter. If B empirically supervenes on A, then it is empirically necessary that no two empirical situations can differ with respect to B without also differing with respect to A (or simply, B cannot vary with the same A). Conceptual supervenience is a stronger notion than empirical supervenience. Indeed, Conceptual supervenience implies empirical supervenience, but I think empirical supervenience is already enough for the sake of my argument in this chapter. Nagel's argument is about sovereignty, and Murphy's argument is about non-ideal political situations. Neither of their arguments is related to other possible worlds.

---

supervenience is a metaphysical notion and roughly includes the attributes, qualities, features, or characteristics of things.

[3] For example, Kim (1993) has also discussed different notions of supervenience such as global, strong, and weak supervenience. However, since his notions of supervenience are not directly related to the debate in this chapter, I do not discuss his notions of supervenience in further detail here.

Monism, Dualism, and Supervenience 37

For example, Nagel does not argue that sovereignty is a necessary condition for assuring justice in every possible world. He simply argues his idea within our actual world. Some philosophers may discuss dualism or monism in a conceptual level, but neither Nagel nor Murphy had done so in their own arguments, and so here I also do not discuss conceptual supervenience, which is a harder and more complicated notion of supervenience. Therefore, while dualists and monists argue whether politics and morality are fundamental or not, I am going to limit the discussion to empirical supervenience but not conceptual supervenience.

How can we put supervenience into the debate between dualism and monism? The answer is that supervenience can be a standard to justify the basic positions of dualism and monism. Moreover, supervenience may even provide a third position other than dualism and monism. Below is an in-depth explanation of each of these answers.

Although supervenience has been mainly used in the discussion of properties in the philosophy of mind and metaphysics, it can also be used for any kind of relationship, such as facts, laws, and principles. Supervenience is a useful concept here because it is also a useful tool to define the relationship between politics and morality. It seems that dualists consider that the relationship between politics and morality is somewhat weaker than supervenience while monism is stronger than supervenience. Dualism should be a view that politics and morality are two different entities; political principles should not apply to individuals and moral principles should not apply to political institutions. According to this inference, dualists probably believe that political principles should not supervene on moral principles and moral principles should not supervene on political principles. Instead, there should be empirically possible situations with identical moral principles but different political principles, or different moral principles but identical political principles. They should be independent from each other. This would be a reasonable interpretation of dualism.

Monism requires a stronger relationship between politics and morality. Monists think that there should only be one set of fundamental principles applying to both individuals and political institutions. Putting supervenience into monism, the correct interpretation is that political principles should supervene on moral principles and moral principles should supervene on political principles. In other words, there should be no two possible situations with identical moral principles but different political principles, and there should be no two possible situations with different moral principles but identical political principles. This is a bi-supervenience relationship; that is, the supervenience relationship goes in both directions (from political principles to moral principles and from moral principles to political principles). Perhaps monism requires an even stronger relationship between politics and morality (e.g., an identical or reductive relationship) than bi-supervenience does, but this bi-supervenience relationship is sufficient for the sake of our discussion.

Traditionally, dualism and monism seem to be mutually exclusive. Only one of them can be right, and it even appears that one of them *must* be right (i.e., they cannot both be wrong). However, if the interpretation above is correct, then there is at least a third alternative— one may argue that only political principles supervene on moral principles.[4] Indeed, I think that this is the correct option. For the remainder of this chapter, I am going to discuss how we can use supervenience to justify Nagel's and Murphy's arguments and why the third option (political principles supervene on moral principles) is better than dualism and monism.

If political principles supervene on moral principles, then there are no two possible situations with identical moral principles but different political principles. However, since the supervenience relationship moves in only one direction, there can be two possible situations with

---

[4] There is another logical alternative, which is that moral principles supervene on political principles. However, I am not going to discuss this option here and I do not recognize anyone who believes in this option.

Monism, Dualism, and Supervenience

different moral principles but either identical or different political principles. In other words, if two situations have different moral principles, then no restriction will apply to those political principles. There are two important points in this interpretation. First, when political principles supervene on moral principles, it means that political principles depend on moral principles, or moral principles determine political principles. Technically, this determination means that when two situations have the same kind of moral principles, then the political principles cannot be different. This is a view similar to monism because it takes moral principles as fundamental in terms of supervenience. In other words, it is a technical interpretation of the fundamental relationship between politics and morality. Second, the relationship of supervenience is not strong enough to require that political principles are also applicable to individuals.

Here is an analogy. Chalmers (1996) argues that biological properties supervene on physical properties. He writes, "For instance, biological properties supervene on physical properties insofar as any two possible situations that are physically identical are biologically identical" (p. 33). However, we still consider biology and physics as two different subjects. For example, we definitely do not think that evolutionism can explain and apply to any physical problem in quantum mechanics. On the other hand, although we do not think that physical properties can *explain* biological properties, we think that biological evolution cannot *violate* physical properties. No matter how a species evolves, we do not expect that the species can violate, say, general relativity. The reason is because biological properties supervene on physical properties.[5]

Chalmers (1996) does not argue that biological laws supervene on physical laws because he thinks that the claim is too strong. He writes: "I am not suggesting that high-level facts and laws are entailed by

---

[5] More precisely, biological properties supervene on physical properties *globally and logically*. Although I am only trying to argue for an empirical supervenience relationship between politics and morality, I do not think that these details will affect the analogy here.

40   *Benedict S. B. Chan*

microphysical laws . . . That would be a strong claim, and although it might have some plausibility if qualified appropriately, the evidence is not yet in" (p. 71). Nevertheless, the analogy here is about the supervenience relationship itself, not about properties or laws. Thus, I consider that this analogy is still an appropriate example. The point of this analogy is to show what a supervenience relationship should be—if B supervenes on A, then B cannot violate A, even though A cannot explain B. Applying this reasoning to the debate in this chapter shows that moral principles cannot *explain* political principles as well, but every political principle cannot *violate* any moral principle. This interpretation respects both ideas that there are fundamental moral principles and independent political principles.

Why should this supervenience interpretation be the correct approach to explain the relationship between politics and morality? The reason is that when we compare the supervenience interpretation with dualism and monism, we find that it has all of their advantages but none of their disadvantages. Murphy would probably argue that Nagel fails to explain why we should not assure justice by all means if we think that justice is such a good virtue. Nagel would probably contend that Murphy fails to explain how he can apply the principles of justice to personal conducts. But the supervenience interpretation does not have these two failures. We can agree with Murphy that justice is a fundamental value and we should assure it by both institutions and individuals. However, this does not mean that we can only allow one set of principles to assure justice. Similar to Nagel, we can still allow that there is a set of just principles for political institutions and there is another set of principles for individuals, and neither set of principles applies to the other. The difference between the supervenience interpretation and dualism is that even though principles of justice are designed to apply in non-ideal situations, the supervenience interpretation can still allow some other compensation from other principles for individual conducts. It is simply that we do not require that principles of justice apply directly to individuals. For that, Murphy

Monism, Dualism, and Supervenience

41

is applying an overly strong requirement for justice. To assure justice, it is not necessary to require that principles of justice *apply* to individuals as well. All we need is that principles of justice for political institutions do not *violate* any individual moral principle. In summary, the supervenience interpretation allows people to assure justice by both institutions and individuals and there can be different sets of principles for political institutions and individuals. In other words, compared with dualism and monism, this supervenience interpretation has their advantages but not their shortcomings. Therefore, the supervenience interpretation should be the best approach in a practical and pragmatic sense. Instead of dualism or monism, we should define the relationship between politics and morality by this supervenience interpretation.

Although integrating supervenience into political philosophy is a new enterprise, I believe that some philosophers' positions are similar or near enough to my interpretation. They do not use the concept of supervenience, but they think that justice is an ultimate or fundamental moral concern, and they think that there should be separated normative principles for political institutions only. Pogge's (2002) institutional cosmopolitanism is one of them.[6] He argues that each individual should have a moral concern for global justice, but he also argues that there should be some normative principles for political institutions (for both states and global institutions). He even argues that our current world is a non-ideal situation, and so first world people, such as citizens of the United States, should compensate other victims who are living under unjust institutional regimes. Murphy (1998) seems to agree with Pogge's (2002) solution, but he categorizes Pogge as a dualist, and so he thinks that Pogge fails to defend institutional cosmopolitanism

---

[6] "Cosmopolitanism holds that all persons stand in certain moral relations to one another. We are required to respect one another's status as ultimate units of moral concern—a requirement that imposes limits on our conduct and, in particular, on our efforts to construct institutional schemes . . . It concerns the nature of the moral constraints to be imposed. An institutional conception postulates certain fundamental principles of social justice. These apply to institutional schemes and are thus second-order principles: standards for assessing the ground rules and practices that regular human interactions" (Pogge, 2002, pp. 169–170).

because it is incompatible with dualism (Murphy, 1998, p. 283n76). I think Murphy categorizes Pogge on the wrong side. Institutional cosmopolitanism can be interpreted as a view that political principles (for both states and global institutions) supervene on moral principles. For that, it is perfectly reasonable for Pogge to argue his view in the way I have just described. In short, the supervenience relationship of politics and morality can be developed as a view to support Pogge or other similar positions.

I admit that the idea discussed in this chapter can be developed further. For example, I realize that there are many other versions of dualism and monism that I have not discussed in this chapter. The papers from Nagel and Murphy are, at most, an example of dualism and an example of monism. I also have not discussed other notions of supervenience (e.g., global and local supervenience, strong and weak supervenience, and conceptual supervenience). Nevertheless, I have provided the first step of integrating supervenience into the debate between monism and dualism and my argument works *prima facie*. McLaughlin and Bennett (2014) think that supervenience "has been invoked in almost every corner of the field [in analytical philosophy]," but the list they provide does not include any item in political philosophy. The idea I have argued in this chapter can be considered as an additional item on their list of the application of supervenience.

REFERENCES

Chalmers, D. (1996). *The Conscious Mind: In Search of a Fundamental Theory*. New York: Oxford University Press.

Hobbes, T. (1651). *Leviathan*. Project Gutenberg. Retrieved from https://en.wikisource.org/wiki/Leviathan.

Kim, J. (1993). *Supervenience and Mind: Selected Philosophical Essays*. Cambridge: Cambridge University Press.

McLaughlin, B., & Bennett, K. (2014). Supervenience. In E. N. Zalta (Ed.), *The Stanford Encyclopedia of Philosophy* (Spring 2014 Ed.). Retrieved from http://plato.stanford.edu/archives/spr2014/entries/supervenience/.

Murphy, L. (1998). Institutions and the Demands of Justice. *Philosophy & Public Affairs*, *27*(4), 251–291.

Nagel, T. (2005). The Problem of Global Justice. *Philosophy & Public Affairs*, 33(2), 113–147.

Pogge, T. (2002). *World Poverty and Human Rights: Cosmopolitan Responsibilities and Reforms*. Cambridge: Polity Press.

Rawls, J. (1999). *A Theory of Justice* (Rev. ed.). Cambridge, MA: Harvard University Press.

In: Ethics
Editor: Miles Ventura

ISBN: 978-1-53613-533-6
© 2018 Nova Science Publishers, Inc.

Chapter 3

THE IMPORTANCE OF ESTABLISHING ETHICS COMMITTEES WITHIN THE HEALTH SECTOR

Jorge Morales Pedraza
Morales Project Consultancy, Vienna, Austria

ABSTRACT

Most hospitals, clinics, and other medical and research medical institutions within the public and private sector established in different countries, are now required to have an ethics committee. In the US and in several other countries, many of these ethics committees provide an ethics consultation service as well. An ethics committee is a group of individuals formed to protect the interests of patients and address moral issues within the health sector in many countries, consisting of different healthcare professionals and non-medical members. Its main responsibilities are to protect the rights, safety, and well-being of human subjects involved in a clinical trial, to provide public assurance of that protection by, among other things, expressing an opinion on the clinical trial protocol to be used, the suitability of the investigators involved in the

46   *Jorge Morales Pedraza*

trial and the adequacy of the facilities, and on the methods and documents to be used to inform trial subjects and obtain their informed consent.

Keywords: ethics committees, ethics consultant, ethics programs, code of ethics, code of practice, ethical policy, ethical guidelines, ethical principles

INTRODUCTION

Most hospitals, clinics, and other medical and research medical institutions are now required to have an ethics committee. In the US and in several other countries, many of these ethics committees provide an ethics consultation service as well[1]. But, what is an ethics committee and why this body is so important for the health sector in many countries? An ethics committee is a group of individuals selected to protect the interests of patients and address moral issues within the health sector of many countries. In the Directive 2001/20/EC[2], an ethics committee is defined as an independent body consisting of different healthcare professionals and non-medical members, whose main

---

[1] An ethics consultant is an expert in ethics who provides ethics consultations and may also serve as an educator to the ethics committee or program. In some healthcare institutions, an ethics consultant provides ethics expertise to workgroups that are addressing systems issues and have the need to better understand the ethics and preferred practices from an ethics perspective. Sometimes in lieu of having an ethics consultant address ethics questions or concerns, the ethics committee will develop a subcommittee to handle these functions. The decision to have an ethics consultant versus a subcommittee rests with the available resources and the expertise of the committee members. It is recommendable to consider asking the advice of an ethics consultant when two conditions are met: a) you perceive that there is an ethical problem in the care of patients, and b) healthcare providers have not been able to establish a resolution that is agreed upon by the patient/surrogate and the clinicians caring for the patient (Pearlman, 2013). Some of the main reasons why doctors seek ethics consultation, even in the case that the issues subject to the consultation are not in all cases ethics issues are, among others, the following: a) to obtain needed help in deciding what to do; b) to identify a practical way of doing what had already been decided should be done; c) to implement a practical solution to the problems identified; d) to obtain reassurance that the correct decision has being made on these problems; e) to face people who might think that the decision was inappropriate; and f) to seek consensus (McLean, 2007).

[2] EC: European Commission.

responsibilities are to protect the rights, safety, and well-being of human subjects involved in a clinical trial; to provide public assurance of that protection by, among other things, expressing an opinion on the clinical trial protocol to be used, the suitability of the investigators involved in the trial and the adequacy of the facilities to be used[3], and on the methods and documents that will be used to inform trial subjects and obtain their informed consent.

The training in legal matters of all members of an ethics committee is an extremely important issue. However, it seems that this issue has been given little attention by those whose proclaimed that its mission is to expand the system of clinical ethics committees in some countries, such as the United Kingdom. An ethics committee must be willing and able to adhere to legal constraints and considerations adopted by the countries where it is constituted. Thus, the focus must be on what might be called "rules of procedure and establishment," which have been dictated by law in some countries, such as Belgium (Meulenbergs et al., 2005).

It is plausible that many of the issues submitted to the ethics committee's attention are essentially practical or legal rather than ethical. However, considerable debate has been generated in the US about whether ethics committees should include lawyers or might even end up usurping the role traditionally occupied by courts of law in this subject. According to Annas (2005), setting an additional bureaucratic entity called "an ethics committee" to make legal pronouncements can only make medicine more legalistic and impersonal. Moreover, encouraging a group of lay people to attempt to practice law makes no

---

[3] Research involving human participants: Is any social science, biomedical, behavioral or epidemiological activity that entails systematic collection or analysis of data with the intent to generate new knowledge, in which human beings: a) are exposed to manipulation, intervention, observation or other interaction with investigators, either directly or through alteration of their environment, or b) become individually identifiable through investigators' collection, preparation or use of biological material or medical or other records (WHO, 2009).

more sense than encouraging a group of lawyers to attempt to perform surgery ... Good ethics committees begin where the law ends."

THE IMPORTANCE OF ESTABLISHING ETHICS COMMITTEES

In many countries, the establishment of ethics committees within hospitals, clinics, and other medical facilities and research medical institutions, is obligatory by law. In the case of Europe, an ethics committee[4] is typically composed of scientists and lay members of physicians, members of the nursing profession, members with legal expertise, a pharmacist, somebody with ethical expertise, a statistician, and at least one representative of a patient organization, among others (Druml et. al., 2009). The main responsibilities of an ethics committee are the following:

- To review proposed studies with human participants to ensure that they conform to internationally and locally accepted ethical guidelines;
- Monitor studies once they have begun and where relevant;
- Take part in follow-up action and surveillance after the end of the research.

Ethics committees have the authority to approve, reject, or stop studies or require modifications to research protocols. They may also perform other functions, such as setting policies or offering opinions on ongoing ethical issues in research studies.

Review of a research study by an ethics committee is required by international ethical standards governing research activities involving

---

[4] Group of individuals who undertake the ethical review of research protocols involving humans.

The Importance of Establishing Ethics Committees ... 49

human participants, as well as by local law in many jurisdictions. In international cooperative research, the review may be required by the laws of the country in which the research is being sponsored, even if it is not required by the host country's own laws. The review of a research study by an ethics committee is also essential, if the researchers intend to publish the results of their investigation, as most medical journals will not publish the results from a research study that has not received the approval of such a committee. It is important to stress that one of the main responsibilities of an ethics committee is to protect potential participants in the research, but it must also consider potential risks and benefits for the community in which the research will be carried out. Its ultimate goal is to promote high ethical standards in research for health (WHO[5], 2009).

Structure and Functions of an Ethics Committee

According to the WHO report (2009), some ethics committees operate within medical research institutions review board, while others operate on a regional or national level. The advantage of ethics committees that operate within medical research institutions, is that they are familiar with the local conditions and can engage in closer monitoring of ongoing research studies. The disadvantage is that the committee may feel inhibited from rejecting or requesting significant changes to research studies, given the institution's financial interest in attracting externally funded research projects. In countries with multiple ethics committees within the health sector, it is important to develop mechanisms to promote consistency and avoid unnecessary duplication of work.

The main functions of an ethics committee include, among others, the following:

---

[5] WHO: World Health Organization.

50 *Jorge Morales Pedraza*

- Identifying and weighing up the risks and potential benefits of the selected research study;
- Evaluating the process and materials (printed documents and other tools) that will be used for seeking participants' informed consent involved in a research study;
- Assessing the recruitment process and any incentives that will be given to participants involved in a research study;
- Evaluating risks to participants' confidentiality (and the related risk of discrimination) and the adequacy of confidentiality protections;
- Examining any other issues that may affect the ethical acceptability of the research study to be carried out.

In international research, the committee represents the interests of the local population. Thus, it should ensure that the participants and their communities will receive fair benefits from the outcome of the approved research studies (WHO, 2009).

Support and Oversight of the Ethics Committee Activities

According to the WHO (2009) report, ethics committees need staff and funding to support their activities. It is not inappropriate to charge research sponsors a fee for review a research proposal by the Ethics Committee, but the fees should be based on the actual costs of the revision process. Funding mechanisms should be designed to ensure that ethics committees and their members, have no financial incentive to approve or reject specific research studies.

Members of an ethics committee should receive training in the international and local ethical and legal standards governing research adopted by the national competent healthcare authorities, as well as in the process the committee uses to review and approve research

The Importance of Establishing Ethics Committees ... 51

protocols, among other subjects. In the case of the non-scientific members of the Ethics Committee, they should be given a brief in the understanding of medical and research methodology sufficient to enable them to participate actively in the committee's discussions. A good knowledge of the social and cultural context within which the ethics committees will carry out its activities is also important. Training should not be a single activity, but instead of an ongoing process, in which all committee members should participate.

Ethics committees should be subject also to ongoing oversight, both to ensure that they are following approved standards and procedures, and to determine whether their actions are improving the ethical quality of the research. Some committees may choose to undergo a formal accreditation process with national or international organizations (WHO, 2009).

Other oversight mechanisms include regional or national meetings for exchanging information about best practices, or partnerships between ethics committees established in different countries. Such committees can also undertake initiatives to assess the impact of the review process on research participants, for example, by soliciting feedback through suggestion boxes or at community meetings, or by sending representatives to study sites to see if the committee's guidance to investigators is being followed (WHO, 2009).

Main Goals of the Ethics Committee

Most ethics committees established in different countries work as an advisory body; they can help patients and families to take informed decisions, and work with healthcare providers to assist them to make complex and difficult decisions. An ethics committee often reviews hospital policies and procedures for the prevention of potential problems that could be faced within these hospitals, and for the reduction of a probable litigation against the institution (Miller, 2003).

The main goals of a traditional ethics committee are, among others, the following:

- To promote the rights of patients;
- To promote shared decision-making between patients (or their surrogates, if the patient is officially incapacitated) and their clinicians;
- To promote fair policies and procedures that maximize the likelihood of achieving good patient-centered outcomes;
- To enhance the ethical environment for healthcare professionals in hospitals, clinics and other medical and research institutions (Pearlman, 2013).

However, more recently, some ethics committees, particularly those affiliated with academic or research institutions within large healthcare systems, have expanded their traditional functions to have more comprehensive ethics programs. They address both clinical and organizational ethics issues. Ethics programs may provide ethics consultations in response to non-clinical ethics questions, identify and remedy systems-level factors that induce or exacerbate ethical problems and/or impede their resolution (often using quality improvement methods), and promote a positive ethics culture throughout medical and research institutions. Thus, the additional goals of expanded ethics programs include:

- Integrating ethics throughout the healthcare institution from the bedside to the boardroom;
- Ensuring that systems and processes do not to interfere with ethical practices;

The Importance of Establishing Ethics Committees ... 53

- Promoting ethical leadership behaviors, such as explaining the values that underlie decisions, stressing the importance of ethics, and promoting transparency in decision-making (Pearlman, 2013).

The Role of Ethics Committee within the Health System

Why is so important to establish an ethics committee within hospitals, clinics, and other medical facilities, including medical research institutions within the health sector in a country and what is their main role? The answer to this question is the following: an ethics committee should be established to ensure that hospitals, clinics, and other medical and research institutions, in which patients are treated following a medical trial protocol, will carry out their activities respecting a group of ethical principles adopted by the competent national healthcare authorities. A comprehensive group of ethical principles can be found in Morales Pedraza (2012).

In the specific field of tissue banking, the approval of an ethics committee is indispensable for the use of human tissues in certain medical treatments, and to review and approved medical trials and research protocols related to:

a) Tissues discarded after surgery;
b) Tissues removed at autopsy;
c) Tissues collected for 'one-off' research projects;
d) Tissues stored in tissue establishment or tissue banks;
e) Tissues transferred to and from medical facilities (Morales Pedraza, 2012).

An ethics committee should be an independent reporting body whose main responsibility should be to ensure the protection of the rights, safety, and well-being of all persons involved in certain medical trials or research medical activities. These activities should be carried out independently, with the aim of maximizing a benefit for individuals and the society, and minimize risk and harm to patients and donors, particularly in the field of tissue transplantation. The review by the Ethics Committee of a research medical project should consider, among other elements, the ethical behavior and outcome of the research; this includes high-impact activities and new forms of research, e.g., co-production. The intensity during the review process should be proportionate to the potential benefits and level of risk of the proposed research or medical trial treatment. The Ethics Committee should determine the degree of risk and potential harm that may be tolerable in relation to the potential benefits (ESRC, 2017).

An ethics committee should provide public assurance of that protection by reviewing and approving standards and underwriting a code of practices suitable to the activities carried out by hospitals, clinics, and other medical or research institutions.

It is important to single out that an ethics committee generally has no authority to impose sanctions on researchers who violate ethical standards, in the conduct of a research involving humans. They may, however, withdraw the approval of a research project, if judged necessary. They should be required to monitor the implementation of an approved research project and its progression, and to report to institutional or governmental authorities any serious or continuing noncompliance with ethical standards in the conduct of the research work. Failure to submit a report to the Ethics Committee should be considered a clear and grave violation of ethical standards. If sanctions become necessary, then they should be directed at the non-compliant researchers or sponsors. They may include fines or suspension of eligibility to receive research funding in the future or to practice their profession during a certain period or indefinitely, among others.

Membership of the Ethics Committee

Ethics committee members usually represent major clinical services and other stakeholders in healthcare delivery. Thus, it is not uncommon for committee members to include clinicians (physicians and nurses) from medicine, surgery, and psychiatry; social workers; chaplains; and community representatives, among others. These committees may also include a quality improvement manager, an individual responsible for the education program at the facility, a lawyer, and at least one individual with advanced training in ethics. This latter representative can come from many disciplines, including philosophy, law, medicine, theology, and anthropology. All members of an ethics committee should take responsibility for learning techniques of ethical analysis and the arguments surrounding most of the ethically charged issues in clinical practice, including legal issues. Some ethics committees allow guests to participate in their meetings, such as health science's students, philosophy graduate students, physician trainees, facilitators, and patient representatives. Guests need to maintain the confidentiality of the information discussed at the meetings, often signing oaths to that effect (Pearlman, 2013).

It is important to ensure the impartiality of the Ethics Committee through carefully nominated members. These members should be selected in a manner that an adequate representation of the community served by the hospitals, clinics, and other medical and research medical institutions within its territory is ensured. All ethics committee should adopt a rotation policy of its members; this means several committee's members should be replaced periodically, with the aim of blending the advantages of experience with those of fresh perspectives (Morales Pedraza, 2012).

On the other hand, all ethics committees should carry out its activities independently of political, institutional, professional, and market influences. Its work should be guided by ethical policy and

56 *Jorge Morales Pedraza*

guidelines, by an ethical code and a code of practices, and by a set of ethical principles approved by the national competent healthcare authorities in the country. In any case, the independence of the research should be maintained, and where conflicts of interest cannot be avoided, they should be made explicit to the Ethics Committee. In this specific case, the Ethics Committee should be able to conduct ethics review in a wholly independent and impartial manner without any conflicts of interest, and with a focus clearly on the ethics of research proposals (ESRC, 2017). Independence can be achieved by the establishment of an ethics committee composed of members from a wide range of disciplines, including external members, within a policy and governance structure that establishes the right of the Ethics Committee to pass opinions free of influence[6].

The establishment of an ethics committee to supervise the routine work of hospitals, clinics, and other medical and research institutions is, without doubt, an adequate mechanism to ensure the respect for the dignity of the persons involved in certain medical trial treatment, the competent review and evaluation of all ethical aspects related to the research projects they receive, and to ensure that their tasks can be executed free from favoritism and influence that could affect their independence. For this reason, countries, institutions, and communities should strive to develop ethics committees and ethical review systems that ensure the broadest possible coverage of protection for potential research participants, and contribute to the highest attainable quality in science and ethics of biomedical research.

States should promote, as appropriate, the establishment of ethics committees at the national, institutional, and local levels that are independent, multidisciplinary, multisectoral, and pluralistic in nature. Ethics committees should also consider during the realization of its activities the principle of justice; this means that the benefits and

---

[6] Ethics Committee that comprise members from only one discipline or a small number of closely related disciplines, may be regarded as too closely aligned with the interests of researchers (ESRC, 2017).

The Importance of Establishing Ethics Committees ... 57

burdens of research and new medical treatment be distributed fairly among all groups and classes within the society, considering age, gender, economic status, culture, and ethnic considerations (WHO, 2000).

The Ethics Committee has a duty to examine the progress in the research or innovative therapy. It should have access to records and be able to confirm that the medical treatment applied to the patients is, in fact, being used for the purpose for which it was approved. Before permitting research medical institutions to carry out research activities involving human patients, Ethics Committee must confirm:

- The validity of the research proposed using human or the medical treatment selected;
- That the objectives of the proposed research or the medical trial treatment to be applied to the patients cannot be achieved in any other way;
- That the researchers or clinicians have the required facilities and skills for carrying out research activities with human or to use the medical treatment selected with all necessary guarantees for the patients.

Ethics committees may call upon, or establish, a standing list of independent consultants, who may provide special expertise to the committee on proposed research protocols. These consultants may be specialists in ethical or legal aspects, specific diseases or methodologies, or they may be representatives of communities, patients, or special-interest groups. Terms of reference for independent consultants should be established by the Ethics Committee (WHO, 2000).

Once the decision to establish an ethics committee is adopted, it members should establish its own working rules defining the frequency of meetings, what will be considered a quorum of members, the elaboration of the decision-making procedures, and the process for the review of decisions adopted, among others. The rules to be adopted by the Ethics Committee should protect the confidentiality of all documents considered by the committee, as well as the content of all its discussions and decisions that were recorded.

In summary, the main requirements for establishing an ethics committee are, among others, the following:

1. Ethics committees should be established in accordance with the applicable laws and regulations of the country, and in accordance with the values and principles of the communities they will serve;
2. Members of ethics committees should be chosen based upon their experience and irreproachable conduct, and should reflect the composition of the community that will serve, within which hospitals, clinics, and other medical or research institutions are working. There should be complete freedom of speech and no constraints caused by unduly lines of reporting within ethics committees;
3. Ethics committees should approve: a) the duration of appointment; b) the policy for the renewal of an appointment; c) the disqualification procedure; d) the resignation procedure; e) the replacement procedure; and f) the quorum requirements, among other relevant procedures;
4. Ethics committees should approve the conditions of appointment. A statement of the conditions of appointment should include the following: a) a member should be willing to publicize his or her full name, profession, and affiliation; b) all reimbursement for work and expenses, if any, within or related to ethics committee activities, should be recorded and made available to the public upon request; c) all members of an ethics committee should sign a confidentiality agreement regarding meeting deliberations, applications, information on research

The Importance of Establishing Ethics Committees ... 59

participants, and related matters; d) in addition, all ethics committees' administrative staff should sign a similar confidentiality agreement;

5. Ethics committees should protect the rights and welfare of all patients. The primary responsibility of each member of this advisory body is to decide, independently, whether in its opinion the conduct of the proposed activity is in line or not with the mandate of the hospital, clinic, or any other medical and research institutions concerned;

6. Medical research institutions that undertake research activities involving humans should ensure that there are adequate resources to establish and/or maintain the work of the Ethics Committees, in accordance with relevant national regulations;

The underlying goals of an ethics committee should be the following:

- To promote the rights of patients:
- To promote shared decision-making between recipients (patients or their families, if the patients are incapacitated), and their clinicians;
- To promote the adoption of fair policies and procedures;
- To promote safe and ethical practices throughout the whole medical process;
- To enhance the ethical scope of healthcare professionals and institutions.

Finally, according to the WHO report (2000), the follow-up procedure to be applied by an ethics committee to an approved research protocol should take the following elements into consideration:

a) The quorum requirements;

b) The review procedure and the communication procedure for follow-up reviews, which may vary from the requirements and procedures for the initial decision on an application;

c) The follow-up review intervals should be determined by the nature and the events of research projects, though each protocol should undergo a follow-up review at least once a year.

d) The following instances or events require the follow-up review of a research study:

- Any protocol amendment likely to affect the rights, safety, and/or well-being of the research participants or the conduct of the research study;
- Serious and unexpected adverse events that could occur related to the conduct of the research study or product, and the response taken by investigators, sponsors, and regulatory agencies;
- Any event or new information that may affect the benefit/risk ratio of the research study;

e) A decision of a follow-up review should be issued and communicated to the applicant, indicating a modification, suspension, or termination of the Ethics Committee's original decision or the confirmation that the decision is still valid;

f) In case of the premature suspension/termination of a research study, the applicant should notify the Ethics Committee of the reasons for suspension/termination; a summary of results obtained in the research study prematurely suspended/terminated should be communicated to the Ethics Committee for its consideration;

g) Ethics committee should receive notification from the applicant at the time of the completion of a research study;

h) Ethics committee should receive a copy of the final summary or report of a research study.

Risks and Benefits

It is important to stress the following: Once a research project has been found scientifically sound, the Ethics Committee should consider whether any known or possible risks to human beings are justified by the expected benefits, direct or indirect, that are foreseen to obtain from the implementation of the research project, and whether the proposed research methods will minimize harm and maximize the benefits. If the proposed research project is scientifically sound and the balance of risks to anticipated benefits is reasonable, the Ethics Committee should then determine whether the procedures proposed for obtaining informed consent, when applicable, are satisfactory and the process equitable. The Ethics Committee is also responsible for ensuring that all other ethical concerns are satisfactorily resolved, both, in principle, and in practice, for keeping records of its decisions, and for taking measures to follow up on the conduct of ongoing research projects (CIOMS-WHO, 2008).

The implementation of any type of research project must be preceded by a scrupulous evaluation of the relationship between the risks and the potential benefits for the participants and/or their communities. This evaluation requires a thorough and up-to-date knowledge of the scientific literature on the main subject of the research study to be implemented. Comparison of the risks and benefits of the research project must avoid two pitfalls:

- Underestimating the risks and/or overestimating the potential benefits, either of which can result in exposing participants to unjustified harm;
- Overestimating the risks and/or underestimating the potential benefits, thereby holding back potentially beneficial research (WHO, 2009).

For an ethics committee to perform an adequate risk/benefit assessment, the level and type of risks to which participants may be exposed must be described in detail in the research protocol, according to the WHO report (2009). Committee members should not, however, base their assessment solely on the information included in the research protocol, but should also actively seek out additional information, consulting experts, and exchanging information with other ethics committees on the research subject, when appropriate.

Quantitative and qualitative evaluation of the risks and benefits for participants and their community presupposes that the members of the ethics committee are properly trained and well-acquainted with the social, cultural, and economic context within which the research project will be implemented. A multidisciplinary approach is essential to the quality of the evaluation, and the composition of the ethics committee must ensure that the required skills are represented. Continuing education for committee's members, together with sharing and critical analysis of experiences with other ethics committees, help considerably in enhancing their skills.

In the field of medical research, there is no such thing as zero risks; however, ethical review of research must contribute to a practical solution to minimize risks and maximize benefits, while ensuring respect for persons and providing the best possible response to the health needs of populations (WHO, 2009).

A summary of the risks and benefits that should be evaluated by an ethics committee is the following:

- The complexity of the notion of risk, as well as the uncertainty of the potential benefits of the research study, make the process of risk/benefit assessment a significant challenge for an ethics committee;

The Importance of Establishing Ethics Committees ...   63

- Risk/benefit assessment does not stop at the individual; it must also consider communities and health systems adopted by the national competent healthcare authorities;
- The risks of a research project are not limited to potential physical harms, but can also include psychological, social, legal, and economic consequences;
- Evaluation of the benefits of a research study must distinguish between direct benefits for the individuals who participate in the study, expected benefits for the community in which the study will take place, and potential benefits to science and the world at large;
- Identifying and evaluating risks and benefits is not a purely scientific endeavor. It requires the involvement of all stakeholders in the research, including investigators, community, and civil-society representatives, lawyers, and health authorities, among others (CIOMS-WHO, 2008).

Documentation and Communication

Every documentation and communication of an ethics committee should be dated, filed, and archived according to written procedures to be adopted by the committee. A statement is required defining the access and retrieval procedure (including authorized persons) for the various documents, files, and archives elaborated and in possession of the Ethics Committee. It is recommended that, in the case of a research study, documents considered by the Ethics Committee be archived for a minimum period of five years following the completion of a research study.

Documents that should be filed and archived include, but are not limited to:

- The constitution, written standing operating procedures (SOPs), and regular (annual) reports on the Ethics Committee activities;
- The curriculum vitae of all Ethics Committee's members;
- A record of all income and expenses of the research and of Ethics Committee activities, including allowances and reimbursements made to the secretariat and committee's members;
- The published guidelines for submission established by the Ethics Committee;
- The agenda of the Ethics Committee's meetings;
- The minutes of the Ethics Committee's meetings;
- One copy of all materials submitted by an applicant for the consideration and approval by the Ethics Committee;
- The correspondence between committee's members and applicants or concerned parties regarding application, decision, and follow-up of a research study;
- A copy of the decision and any advice or requirements sent by the Ethics Committee to an applicant;
- All written documentation received during the follow-up of the research study approved;
- The notification of the completion, premature suspension or termination of a research study;
- The final summary or report of the research study (WHO, 2009).

CONFIDENTIALITY IN MEDICAL PRACTICES

According to WHO (2009), the ethical principle of confidentiality, already mentioned in the Hippocratic Oath, forms a cornerstone of the relationship between the patient and his or her physician. While the relationship between researchers and research subjects is different from the traditional physician/patient relationship, protecting confidentiality remains an important goal for both.

Confidentiality is an important subject within medical ethics and a relevant issue to build up trust, allowing individuals to reveal all information necessary to treat their medical condition, no matter how sensitive it may be, without having to fear public disclosure. This trust is paramount not only in guaranteeing appropriate medical treatment, but also in protecting public health, as untreated conditions may pose a significant threat to other persons. The obligation of non-disclosure of the health condition of a participant is protected by law in many countries.

Participation in medical research may lead to information disclosure that could have a negative impact on the participant and/or his or her family and community. Therefore, all personal information must be safeguarded, whether the researcher and participants are in a formal physician/patient relationship. This applies even to personal information that in the physicians and/or researcher's opinion would not consider as particularly sensitive for the participant. In certain circumstances, physicians and/or researchers may be permitted or even required, to reveal confidential information, particularly in legal cases. Generally, these involve situations in which an individual poses an immediate danger to third parties, such as when mentally ill patients make credible threats of violence against specific individuals.

What kind of information should be safeguarded? All personal information from a patient must be safeguarded. Personal information includes all information "relating to an identified or identifiable natural person (data subject)[7] (Directive 95/46/EC, 1995).

The information by which an individual can be identified includes, but is not limited, to the following:

---

[7] An identifiable person is one who can be identified, directly or indirectly, by reference to an identification number or to one or more factors specific to his physical, physiological, mental, economic, cultural or social identity."

- Name;
- Social security number;
- Address;
- Phone number;
- Any other information that reveals that an individual is a member of a small group of people, such as the information that a person works in an office or lives in a specific apartment building; a combination of information, such as physical appearance, date of birth and place of work, that together can reveal the individual's identity (Directive 95/46/EC, 1995).

Ways to Minimize Confidentiality Risks

A summary of the ways that can be used by an ethics committee to minimize the confidentiality risks is the following:

- Only collect data that can lead to the identification of research participants, if this information is necessary for the successful completion of the research project. In some cases, confidentiality risks can be avoided by not collecting any identifiable information;
- When identifiable information must be collected, consider replacing individuals' names with code numbers and storing the key to the code in a secure location accessible only to a limited number of persons defined by the Ethics Committee. Destroy the key code when it is no longer necessary to link data with identities for research. If linkable information (that is, potentially identifiable data) is held, the purpose of this storage, its duration, and the persons which will be granted access to it, must be made explicit by a decision of the Ethics Committee;

- Increase researchers' awareness of confidentiality issues by providing periodically guidance and training;
- Ensure that information is secured by limiting access, using safe storage methods (e.g., locked drawers and password-protected computer access) and using protected means of communication (e.g., encrypted electronic messages);
- Destroy information as soon as it is no longer needed (WHO, 2009).

CONCLUSION

The establishment of ethics committees in hospitals, clinics, and other medical facilities and research medical institutions is already a common practice in many countries, and is regulated by specific laws and regulations in most of them. The composition, functioning, and responsibilities of such committees must follow the regulations in force in the countries where they are established, as well as the ethical principles and other regulations that have been adopted at the regional and international level on the subject.

It is very important that ethics committees can function free of political pressure and that their members can exercise their right to express freely their opinions and criteria on all matters that are submitted to their consideration. National competent healthcare authorities should ensure that the ethics committees that have been established, have the financial resources to carry out their activities without artificial restrictions.

Undoubtedly, the activities of an ethics committee should ensure respect for the rights of participants in research studies that are approved or the rights of patients to undergo experimental medical treatments. These must participate in such research and treatments in a totally voluntary manner, and should be free from all types of pressure

68   *Jorge Morales Pedraza*

from the researchers or the medical personnel involved in them. Participants should feel that their presence in this research and treatment has as a fundamental objective to significant improve their quality of life and that the benefits expected to be obtained are far superior to the possible risks that could be faced.

REFERENCES

Annas G, J. (2005); Ethics committees: from ethical comfort to ethical cover; *Hastings Cent Rep* 19912118–21; 2005.

Directive 95/46/EC of the European Parliament and of the Council of 24 October 1995 on the protection of individuals with regard to the processing of personal data and on the free movement of such data (http://europa.eu/scadplus/leg/en/lvb/l14012.htm, accessed 18 January 2009.

Druml, Christiane; Wolzt, M. J.; Singer, Pleiner E. A. (2009); Research ethics committees in Europe: trials and tribulations, *Legal and ethical issues in clinical research*, 2009.

International Ethical Guidelines for Epidemiological Studies (2008); Council for International Organizations of Medical Sciences (CIOMS) in collaboration with the World Health Organization (WHO); CIOMS; Geneva; Switzerland; February 2008.

McLean, Sheila A. M. (2007); What and who are clinical ethics committees for? *Journal of Medical Ethics*; DOI: 10.1136/jme. 2007.021394, 2007.

Meulenbergs T.; Vermylen J.; and Schotsmans P. T. (2005); The current state of clinical ethics and healthcare ethics committees in Belgium; *J Med Ethics* 200531318–321; 2005.

Miller-Keane Encyclopaedia and Dictionary of Medicine, Nursing, and Allied Health, Seventh Edition; Elsevier; 2003.

Morales Pedraza, Jorge (2012); *The Use of the Ionizing Radiation Technique for Tissue Sterilization: The International Atomic Energy Agency Experience*; Nova Science; ISBN 978-161324-368-8; 2012.

Operational Guidelines for Ethics Committees That Review Biomedical Research (2000); WHO, TDR/PRD/ETHICS/2000.1; Geneva, Switzerland; 2000.

Our principles: research ethics committees (2017); Economic and Social Research Council (ESRC); 2017.

Pearlman, Robert A. (2013); *Ethics Committees, Programs, and Consultation*; Department of Bioethics & Humanities, and Department of Health Services, University of Washington and the VA Puget Sound Health Care System; 2013.

Research ethics committees. *Basic concepts for capacity-building* (2009); World Health Organization (WHO); ISBN 978 92 4 159800 2; 2009.

In: Ethics
Editor: Miles Ventura

ISBN: 978-1-53613-533-6
© 2018 Nova Science Publishers, Inc.

Chapter 4

THE CONVERGENCE OF TECHNOLOGIES IN HEALTHCARE: NEW CHALLENGES FOR BIOETHICS

Pamela Tozzo, MD, PhD and Luciana Caenazzo, PhD[*]
Department of Molecular Medicine, University of Padova,
Padova, Italy

ABSTRACT

During the last two decades new forms and types of technologies have emerged: some examples include nanotechnology, neuroscience/ neurotechnology, and many converging technologies that combine bio- and nanotechnology with physical sciences. In this chapter we will address some bioethical issues raised by the convergence of these new technologies.

The technological convergence reinforces the development of the technologies involved, creating new application domains by their combination, with an important influence in medical sciences.

---

[*] Corresponding Author Email: pamela.tozzo@gmail.com.

In this developing field, we can distinguish among different pathways, but particularly in the field of public health we see different emerging projects regarding record-linkage between *Big Data* archives of various origins (commercial, economic, institutional, social networks, etc.) resulting in the definition of subsets of the population to be considered at higher risk of developing a particular disease, and record-linkage between electronic administrative health archives, which could be processed using disease-specific algorithms to identify individuals with disease in a population.

The increasingly widespread use of digital recording in administrative, commercial and social networks is opening up new and unpredictable scenario which might also influence the definition of disease in a digital society. Some Authors have addressed this issue, examining the feasibility of record linking between health-related archives and other electronic archives such as Facebook, Twitter, blogs, online shopping habits, GPS recordings of individual mobility, personal devices monitoring physical exercise, and so on. By developing appropriate algorithms, it would be possible to identify subsets of the population at higher risk of developing diseases, to ascertain whether distances between homes and drugstores or hospitals influence people's health profiles, to see whether the characteristics shared by Facebook friends influence their individual health profiles, and so on. The possibilities related to the use of this data are limitless, and inevitably give rise to ethical aspects related to the value of data, privacy concerns, consent, and population health priorities and related needs, management of prevention campaigns, public health intervention planning and resource allocation.

Keywords: converging technologies, *Big Data*, personal health data, ethical issues

1. INTRODUCTION

Today (bio)-technologies play a significant role in many areas fundamental to human wellbeing, including food and energy production, medicine and industry. Although they have been responsible for substantial benefits, the historical impact of biotechnologies on human wellbeing has not been uniformly positive. Nevertheless, as a society we place significant investment in

The Convergence of Technologies in Healthcare 73

prospective biotechnologies to increase future wellbeing, while at the same time we are still providing remedies for the accumulated negative impacts of previous technologies.

At the dawn of the 21st century, some researchers have perceived the emergence of a phenomenon in science and technology: the convergence of technologies as a process of bringing together knowledges, practices, products and applications into productive conjunctions. This is a complex process highly dependent on the development and innovation context and not merely on the quality of the underlying science. The term "converging technologies" refers to the synergistic combination of four major "NBIC" (nano-bio-info-cogno) provinces of science and technology, each of which is currently progressing at a rapid rate: (a) nanoscience and nanotechnology; (b) biotechnology and biomedicine, including genetic engineering; (c) information technology, including advanced computing and communications; (d) cognitive science, including cognitive neuroscience. Singly, each of them has a large potential to change society and mankind, but combined they represent a still more powerful source for even bigger change. In converging, the synergy of developments in these different technologies may greatly increase their applications and/or may create new applications domains by combining nano- and biotechnology, information and communication technology and cognitive science (van Est et al., 2014).

Convergence describes transformative processes that lead to the creation of something novel beyond the sum of those aspects that are converging: knowledge practices, stakeholders, artefacts or spaces. Convergence does not simply equate to disciplinary synergy, and encompasses more than knowledges and skills (Wienroth and Rodrigues, 2015).

The capacity of converging technologies to produce profound changes in our social, commercial or physical environments, may have significant implications for shared ways of life, not only for the 'users' of those technologies, but for all members of society. These are not merely technical or economic impacts, but also medical, social and ethical ones. The potentially pervasive and irreversible nature of such transformations underscores the importance of opening up reflection about ethics implications that may arise.

The potential of converging technologies to create significant benefits and harms may originate not only from intended uses but also as a result of misuse, leading to unintended consequences and associated uncertainties and ambiguities. These potential harms often occur at a public scale from which individuals cannot 'opt out' or be excluded. Potential harms may also be public harms, either direct (e.g., the accidental release of an engineered pathogen) or indirect (e.g., exacerbated social inequality). In some cases, biotechnologies may be different from other technologies in that their effects are mediated through complex biological and ecological systems that may have widespread, exponential, or long term consequences. While not necessarily of greater magnitude or longevity than the adverse effects of other technologies (as, for example, a nuclear accident), the complexity of the biological systems in which they operate, and the obscurity of the real underpinning mechanisms, can make these effects harder to conceive, predict and to control (Nuffield Council of Bioethics, 2012).

With proper attention to ethical issues and societal needs, converging technologies could achieve a tremendous improvement in human abilities, societal outcomes, the nation's productivity, and the population's quality of life. This is a broad, cross-cutting, emerging and timely opportunity of interest to individuals, society and humanity in the long term. It is therefore evident that the balance between public interest and individual rights becomes more significant nowadays than in the past, as for example in the field of biobanking (Caenazzo et al., 2015).

Health information is involved in these forms of converging technologies as well; patients are gathered through "Information Technologies" (IT) that assemble information and constitute forms of aggregation of *Big Data*. Moreover, the possibility to assemble different information allows expanding the potentiality of the original data archives.

2. NEW OPPORTUNITIES AND CHALLENGES FOR RESEARCH

Consumer-oriented electronic devices, apps, and services are now able to capture a variety of parameters directly relevant to human health. Advances in microtechnology, data processing and storage, wireless communication and networking infrastructure, and battery capacity have resulted in the proliferation of devices that have made it possible for individuals to produce ever-larger streams of data across the lifespan, throughout the course of health and illness, and in a geospatial context. The current technological revolution generated by the increasingly connection to the world of digital information puts people in the position of generating enormous amounts of data through the widespread use of such devices.

Applications designed to collect, store, and analyze these Personal Health Data (PHD) have proliferated and are increasingly being used by a wide range of individuals for self-tracking. In early 2013, the Pew Research Center's Tracking for Health study found that 69% of Americans track some form of health-related information and 21% use a digital device to do so. In addition to self-tracked PHD, more and more data about individuals are being captured passively as people surf the web, communicate with one another on social networks, make financial transactions, or conduct other activities that leave "digital footprints" (Bietz et al., 2016).

Nearly all of the electronic devices, apps, and services that collect and store PHD are outside the mainstream of traditional health care or public health research. This includes everything from small start-ups to globally active consumer electronics, telecommunications, and search-oriented or social network corporations. Concurrently, there seems to be an increasing willingness for individuals to share their PHD with others. This can be seen in the Quantified Self Movement, where individuals meet to share insights gained from their self-tracking activities. Additionally, many people now share their data with those who have similar medical conditions in the context of online groups such as MIDATA (https://www.midata.coop/), PatientsLikeMe (https://www.patientslikeme.com/) or Crohnology (https://crohnology.com/).

The growing amount of PHD presents an opportunity to move beyond the use of population-level data for simple descriptive epidemiology to its use for making causal inferences (Simonato et al., 2016). What we should bear in mind when facing with this developing way of creating and storing healthcare data is that most people are more prone to find, share, receive health and medical information than in the past. This data are numerous, they cannot be easily categorized into regular health databases and, most importantly, they are generated, captured and processed very quickly.

These new methods of acquiring data and approaching research raise new challenges but also renown issues, including data access, privacy, and consent. Privacy norms and expectations are becoming more diverse, stretched in opposite directions by opposing trends. On one hand, sharing is common in an era of online communication and social networking sites like Facebook, Twitter, and Pinterest. On the other hand, there may be increased desire for attention to privacy as a result of adverse media events.

Closely related to privacy is the need for informed consent in order to maintain public trust in the research enterprise. For researchers, data access becomes complicated when researchers acquire data from third parties rather than collect it directly. The scientific method is based on

The Convergence of Technologies in Healthcare 77

full transparency in data generation, manipulation, and analysis. Entities with a vested interest in protecting their intellectual property may refuse to share their proprietary software and algorithms, making it difficult, if not impossible, to interpret the data, establish its validity, and replicate research. Whereas *Big Data* technologies in physics and genomics were largely developed by academics, almost all of the resources relevant to PHD are commercially developed and are subject to a variety of intellectual property and licensing restrictions.

Health information is of particular interest in the epidemiological sphere since it is related to a population size that can take on significant dimensions, for example metropolitan longitudinal studies are already based on data contained in numerous health and non-data files, and more and more, in the coming years, will be overwhelmed by a plethora of data coming from a wide variety of new sources - including the large volumes of low-cost molecular OMIC data and by continuous monitoring and sometimes at a distance of countless sensors (for example data collected by Smartphones and GPS). Dealing with such *Big Data* will necessarily require new approaches to access, manipulation and display of multimodal information: this will lead to a completely new perspective on data management, but that will also have enormous opportunities, particularly in decision-making for stratified or personalized healthcare.

This new way of doing research, through the use and management of this huge amount of data, has been accompanied by the development of new ethical, practical and standard rules, especially regarding the issue of consent. Despite innovations in using technology to develop new research capabilities, the ability to use technology to address some of the ethical and legal issues related to participation in biomedical research has not been fully realized.

3. OLD CHALLENGES FOR NEW TECHNOLOGIES: OWNERSHIP, PRIVACY AND CONSENT

Taken together, there appear to be many opportunities for, and considerable enthusiasm about, the potential for leveraging PHD for health research. Challenges to the use of PHD for health research were identified in the following areas: data ownership and data access for research, privacy, informed consent, research methods and data quality and issues related to an evolving set of devices, apps, and other services that leave "digital footprints."

Although individuals usually express concern about maintaining their privacy, they convey considerable willingness to have their PHD shared with and used by researchers. Their main concerns are related to the possible commercial uses of their PHD, to which many had an aversion. Both researchers and companies noted that even when there is general willingness to share PHD, accomplishing this can be an arduous task due to regulatory and legal constraints.

Creating the right contract language, material transfer agreements, or other documentation that satisfies both corporate counsel as well as the research partners is challenging. There is a need for new technology and policy solutions that ease the movement of data between companies and researchers while protecting the rights of individuals. Other strategies include advancing and fostering the adoption of language for data use agreements and terms of service that make it easier for companies to respond if a customer desires to make their data available for research.

Policies and practices that relate to privacy protection in the management of health information in the era of medical records, clinical trials, and periodic public health surveys may be insufficient at this time when more and more PHD are being produced. Users of self-tracking technologies are frequently unaware of the details of data access to which they agree in the context of clicking "accept" to terms

The Convergence of Technologies in Healthcare 79

of use. Even with an awareness of data access issues and permissions, it is often difficult to predict effects on privacy. For example, while data may be anonymized before being shared, there is a very real risk of revealing a person's identity if two or more sources of personal data are combined. In this unsettled policy and technology environment, there is also little understanding of the nature and degree of actual risks, if any, associated with re-identification and/or other breaches of PHD privacy.

Several activities that specifically address recommendations about how to handle privacy issues for PHD might help protect the availability of these forms of data for research aimed at improving the public good (Morrison et al., 2016).

First, additional research is needed to help to unpack and understand user expectations regarding the privacy of their PHD. This understanding can then help inform conversations aimed at establishing norms of use. Second, there is a need to develop appropriate education and outreach materials to help in discussions about the realities and challenges of digital anonymity. Third, tools need to be developed to enhance user control of data, awareness of sharing, and notification of findings derived from the use of PHD in research. These controls are an essential condition for establishing the trust needed to assure that data donation is not a one-time occurrence.

Just as these new forms of data raise new questions about data privacy, they also create new questions for the ethics of research, particularly in the field of consent. Most of the current framing of research ethics comes from a pre-digital era. The very characteristics that make PHD valuable for research also make it ethically challenging (Nuffield Council on Bioethics, 2015). PHD provides a high level of detail about the everyday activities of individuals. Large amounts of data can be collected at relatively low cost, and many of the sensors and digital traces are generated without active engagement (or even awareness) by participants (McWhirter et al., 2014). The same devices and apps that generate PHD are also platforms for delivering information to users, providing an opportunity for intervention experiments with a sample size that was previously impractical, if not impossible. While some academic communities have considered these issues and developed ethics guidelines for internet research, there does not appear to be broad awareness or adoption of such recommendations in health research or by IRBs. There is a need for high-level, interdisciplinary efforts to revisit fundamental ethics principles, consider how they apply to these new modalities of research, and update the procedures and recommendations that guide researchers and IRBs (Strand and Kaiser, 2015). Simultaneously, there is an opportunity for experimentation with new models and technologies of informed consent, de-identification, and trusted sharing that can balance respect for the individual with the scientific potential of PHD.

These transformations are reconfiguring traditional boundaries between: patient, research participant and consumer; lay people and experts; medical research and clinical practice; and between the public and private domains. New configurations of technologies, service providers and users challenge existing regulatory categories, present novel opportunities and risks, and raise important ethical questions (Caenazzo et al., 2017). Increased sharing of personal medical and biological information and increasingly international movements of data raise issues of privacy and security, but also challenge the adequacy of traditional ethical concepts like consent, and, indeed, justice. Many large scale data gathering operations rely on a broad consent for using and re-using data for multiple purposes. This concept challenges established understandings of what informed consent is intended to mean, and raises the possibility that the protections it is supposed to offer may be undermined. Similarly, global and networked flows of data are also redefining the meaning of other traditional protections of human subjects' research such as the right to withdraw from participation. What are the implications of these changes for public trust and accountability in research? What governance options are afforded, and which capabilities are required, by the digital and algorithmic processing of data on a global scale? And is there a danger that the increasing focus on individual biological and life-style causes of disease might overshadow efforts to address environmental and systemic determinants of illness?

As translational endeavours foster new kinds of engagement between doctors, scientists, patients, citizens, states and companies it is important to consider how this affects what it means to be engaged in research. It is particularly relevant to consider the impact of these changes on populations who are already marginalised or under-represented in medical research. This applies not only to different communities within developed countries, but to the wider flow of data, materials, technology and medical knowledge between the global North and South.

4. MOVING A STEP FORWARD: THE RIGHT TO BE FORGOTTEN

Properly balancing compensation risks and the maintenance of privacy in data is presently one of the greatest challenges posed by electronic *Big Data* management.

People who sign in to social media sites are typically opted in automatically, allowing their data to be collected and shared. The will to want to be forgotten after leaving traces online, on social networks or by recording personal data/events through the applications of the most common electronic devices, can obviously also concern health data.

The generic life cycle of scientific data is composed of sequential stages, including research project, data collection and processing, discussion, feedback and archiving (Khan et al., 2014). Large amounts of data are stored in web platforms, but customers usually cannot directly check the outsourced data, for example in case of transmission and dissemination within countries, program monitoring and use by international organization.

This situation clearly pose the problematic balance between privacy and the risk of unprincipled data misuse, leading to forms of inequity, stigmatization and limited freedom. In this context it is of paramount importance to connect a legal and ethical concept, that is privacy, to a technical concept that is data security, reached through technical approaches that address issues covering physical, electronic and procedural aspects of protecting information collected.

The Italian Committee for Bioethics in the document "The Identification of The Human Body: Bioethical Aspects of Biometrics", paragraph "The right to oblivion," reports: "Memory is a key element of individual identity and social relations. It is difficult to imagine any internal development and cultural progress without the conservation and organization of traces of the past, which may take many forms: memory, history, opinion, prejudice, etc.). Oblivion is just as important to make a selection within this set of elements, avoiding any unnecessary or harmful accumulation. To ensure social stability and to protect individuals' fundamental rights and freedoms, juridical experience has had to develop artificial forms of oblivion (despite their diversity: removal from criminal records, prescription, amnesty, pardon, etc.), where morality entrusts to forgiveness the extreme inner effort to overcome the past." (Italian Committee for Bioethics, 2010). In the context of PHD "avoiding any unnecessary or harmful accumulation" should be considered on two levels: the storage of biological samples, and the storage of data referring to each individual. In May 2014 the European Court of Justice ruled that the right to be forgotten "requires the search engine to remove links to pages that appear to be inadequate, irrelevant or no longer relevant or excessive … in the light of the time that had elapsed." (European Court of Justice, 2014).

The principle of "the right to be forgotten," which has so far been dealt with internationally from the point of view of the right of a citizen to redemption and forgiveness, can also be applied within the framework of electronic health data. Some information, and especially those related to transient pathological changes (for example neoplasms that usually bring high emotional impact), may become, after a period of time adequate to use them for retrospective epidemiology research, irrelevant, or useless or even inaccurate, both for the research and the single patient. In these cases, the patient, as well as the person guilty of having committed a crime for which he has paid his debt and has been redeemed, may feel that he no longer wants to be tied or relayed to that information, which may have been, in the past, cause of suffering, difficulty, discrimination. In other words, respect for the right to be forgotten can be a form of overcoming, for the patient, some phases of illness the patient first no longer wants to remember.

Appropriate policies, possibly shared among different countries, security procedures and technical methods – concerning how data are collected, stored, exchanged and eventually released – should be balanced to protect both individual and public rights, that is to say, on the one hand, the right of a citizen not to leave infinitely recoverable traces of his healthcare-oriented web searches, recordings of health records or web sharing on his own experience of illness and, on the other, the incommensurable potency to collect and organize these data consciously in order to set epidemiological or health prevention policies out of the extraordinary effectiveness.

A number of organizational procedures should be developed to ensure safeguards for the collection, transfer, storage, use, dissemination and disposal of personal identified data and other information related to health data obtained from convergence of technologies.

CONCLUSION

Obtaining relevant data within huge amounts of health data coming from electronic devices is a critical issue. Big amount of electronic health data are important for health care improvement, and are accumulating increasingly. While there are several ongoing efforts to represent and structure it seems that addressing similar concerns by drawing attention to the lack of regulatory oversight of unauthorized secondary uses of health data and samples is still missing. Creative solutions must be found that allow individual rights to be respected while providing access to high-quality and relevant PHD for research, that balance open science with intellectual property, and that enable productive and mutually beneficial collaborations between the private sector and the academy. A great deal of experimentation is taking place that is working toward these goals. Findings from this project suggest that the public good can be served by these advances, but that there is also work to be done to ensure that policy, legal, and technological developments enhance the potential to generate knowledge out of PHD, and ultimately, improve health and well-being.

REFERENCES

Bietz, MJ; Bloss, CS; Calvert, S; Godino, JG; Gregory, J; Claffey, MP; Sheehan, J; Patrick, K. Opportunities and challenges in the use of personal health data for health research. *Journal of the American Medical Informatics Association*, 2016 23, e42-8.

Caenazzo, L; Tozzo, P; Borovečki, A. Ethical governance in biobanks linked to electronic health records. *European Review for Medical and Pharmacological Sciences,* 2015 19, 4182-4186.

Caenazzo, L; Mariani, L; Pegoraro, R. *Convergence of New Emerging Technologies. Ethical challenges and new responsibilities.* Padova: Piccin; 2017.

European Court of Justice. *Factsheet on the "Right to be Forgotten" ruling* (C-131/12). 2014 June 3rd. Available from: http://ec.europa.eu/justice/data-protection/files/factsheets/factsheet _data_protection_en.pdf.

The Convergence of Technologies in Healthcare 85

Khan, N; Yaqoob, I; Hashem, IA; Inayat, Z; Ali, WK; Alam, M; Shiraz, M; Gani, A. Big Data: survey, technologies, opportunities, and challenges. *Scientific World Journal*, 2014 2014, 712826.

Italian Committee for Bioethics. *The identification of the human body: bioethical aspects of biometrics*. 2010 Nov 26th. Available from: http://bioetica.governo.it/media/171906/p95_2010_identification-human-body_en-cnb.epub.

McWhirter, RE; Critchley, CR; Nicol, D; Chalmers, D; Whitton, T; Otlowski, M; Burgess, MM; Dickinson, JL. Community engagement for big epidemiology: deliberative democracy as a tool. *Journal of personalized medicine*, 2014 4, 459-74.

Morrison, M; Dickenson, D; Lee, SS. Introduction to the article collection 'Translation in healthcare: ethical, legal, and social implications.' *BMC Medical Ethics*, 2016 17, 74.

Nuffield Council on Bioethics. *Emerging biotechnologies: technology, choice and the public good*. London: Nuffield Council on Bioethics; 2012.

Nuffield Council on Bioethics. *The collection, Linking and use of data in biomedical research and health care: ethical issues*. 2015. Available from: http://nuffieldbioethics.org/project/biological-health-data.

Simonato, L; Baldo, V; Canova, C; Pegoraro, R. The uncertain definition of diseases in the light of emerging technologies. *Clinical Research & Bioethics*, 2016 7, 1-4.

Strand, R; Kaiser, M. *Report on Ethical Issues Raised by Emerging Sciences and Technologies*. Report written for the Council of Europe, Committee on Bioethics. 2015 Jan 23rd. Available from: https://rm.coe.int/168030751d

van Est, R; Stemerding, D; Rerimassie, V; Schuijff, M; Timmer, J; Brom, F. *From Bio to NBIC convergence –From Medical Practice to Daily Life*. Report written for the Council of Europe, Committee on Bioethics. The Hague, The Netherlands: Rathenau Instituut; 2014.

Wienroth, M; Rodrigues, E. *Knowing New Biotechnologies. Social aspects of technological convergence*. New York: Routledge; 2015.

INDEX

#

20th century, 2
21st century, 2, 3, 15, 73

A

access, 57, 63, 66, 67, 76, 77, 78, 84
accountability, 80
accreditation, 51
adverse effects, 74
adverse event, 60
advisory body, 51, 59
aggregation, 75
anthropology, 55
applied ethics, 8, 16
appointment, 58
Aristotle, 6, 10
arithmetic, 7, 17
artificial intelligence, 8
assessment, 62, 63
atrocities, 21
attitudes, 7, 21
attribution, 4, 20

authority(ies), 11, 19, 20, 28, 29, 48, 50, 53, 54, 56, 63, 67
aversion, 7, 78
awareness, 5, 8, 67, 79
axiology, 7

B

banking, 53
Belgium, 47, 68
benefits, 17, 49, 50, 54, 56, 61, 62, 63, 68, 72, 74
Big Data, x, 72, 75, 77, 81, 85
bioethics, 8
biological samples, 82
biological systems, 74
biotechnology, 73
bridge, 16, 17

C

calculus, 7, 17, 18
campaigns, xi, 72
causal inference, 76
challenges, 10, 76, 79, 80, 81, 84, 85

88 *Index*

Chalmers, 36, 39, 42, 85
chaplains, 55
China, 25
Christian ethics, 2, 10, 17
Christianity, 11
citizens, 28, 29, 33, 41, 81
civic virtues, 19
civil society, 11
civil war, 31
clinical trial protocol, ix, 45, 47
clinical trials, 78
clinicians, 46, 52, 55, 57, 59
code of ethics, 46
code of practice(s), 46, 54, 56
codes of conduct, 13
cognition, 8
cognitive science, 73
collaboration, 68
commercial, viii, x, 72, 73, 78
communication, 60, 63, 67, 73, 75, 76
communist countries, 15
communities, 50, 56, 57, 58, 61, 63, 80, 81
community, 6, 9, 12, 49, 51, 55, 58, 62, 63, 65
community representatives, 55
compensation, 40, 81
complexity, 62, 74
compliance, 11
composition, 58, 62, 67
conception, 28, 41
confidentiality, 13, 50, 55, 58, 64, 66, 67
consent, xi, 72, 76, 77, 79, 80
consequentialism, 7
conservation, 82
constitution, 64
consulting, 62
consumer ethics, 8
contingency, 29
contradiction, 14
controversial, 7, 32
convergence, viii, x, 3, 10, 71, 73, 83, 86
convergence of technologies, viii, 73, 83

converging technologies, x, 71, 72, 73, 74
corruption, 11, 15
cosmopolitanism, 41
Council of Europe, 85, 86
critical analysis, 62
cultural conditions, 21
cultural differences, 3
culture, viii, 1, 2, 5, 7, 20, 21, 52, 57

D

danger, 14, 65, 80
data archives, 75
data collection, 81
data gathering, 80
data generation, 77
data processing, 75
death penalty, 7
defects, 10
democracy, viii, 2, 4, 85
deontology, 2, 12, 19
depth, vii, viii, 25, 26, 30, 37
descriptive ethics, viii, 2, 8, 14
developed countries, 81
deviant behaviour, 13
discipline-specific ethics, 12
disclosure, 65
discordance, viii, 2
discrimination, 50, 83
diseases, viii, x, 57, 72, 85
dissonance, 14
distribution, 27, 31, 33
distributive justice, vii, viii, 25, 26, 27, 28, 30, 34, 35
divergence, 3, 7, 10
diversity, 3, 82
doctors, 46, 81
documentation, 63, 64, 78
dualism, v, vii, viii, 25, 26, 27, 28, 30, 31, 32, 33, 35, 37, 38, 40, 42

Index

89

E

ecological systems, 74
economic consequences, 63
economic status, 57
education, 3, 11, 20, 21, 32, 55, 62, 79
egoism, 18
elaboration, 58
emergency, 18
empathy, 14
environment, 16, 47, 52, 79
environmental ethics, 7, 8
epidemiology, 76, 83, 85
epistemology, 6
equality, 27, 29, 32
ethical analysis, 55
ethical code, 11, 56
ethical discourse, 3
ethical education, 21
ethical formalism, 12
ethical guidelines, 46, 48
ethical issues, 48, 68, 72, 74, 85
ethical policy, 46, 55
ethical principles, 46, 53, 56, 67
ethical standards, 13, 48, 54
ethics, v, vii, viii, ix, 1, 2, 3, 5, 6, 7, 8, 9, 10,
    11, 12, 13, 14, 15, 16, 17, 18, 19, 20, 21,
    23, 33, 35, 45, 46, 47, 48, 49, 50, 51, 52,
    53, 54, 55, 56, 57, 58, 59, 60, 61, 62, 63,
    64, 65, 66, 67, 68, 69, 74, 79, 85
ethics committees, ix, 45, 46, 47, 48, 49, 50,
    51, 52, 55, 56, 58, 59, 62, 67, 68, 69
ethics consultant, 46
ethics programs, 46, 52
Europe, 2, 7, 48, 68
European Commission, 46
European Court of Justice, 82, 84
European Parliament, 68
euthanasia, 7
everyday life, 9, 11, 16
evidence, 40

evil, vii, viii, 2, 3, 4, 5, 6, 7, 10, 11, 15, 16,
    21
evolution, 4, 39
evolutionism, 39
exercise, 67
expertise, 16, 46, 48, 57

F

Facebook, viii, x, 72, 76
facilitators, 55
fairness, 27, 30
faith, 5, 12
families, 51, 59
financial, 49, 50, 67, 75
financial resources, 67
freedom, 4, 5, 12, 58, 82
funding, 50

G

general ethics, 9
genetic engineering, 73
genetic factors, 3
genocide, 20
genomics, 77
global ethics, 8
global scale, 80
good, vii, viii, 2, 3, 4, 5, 6, 7, 9, 10, 11, 13,
    15, 16, 20, 21, 31, 34, 40, 51, 52, 79, 84,
    85
governance, 27, 56, 80, 84
governments, 29, 31
GPS, x, 72, 77
graduate students, 55
guidance, 51, 67
guidelines, 46, 48, 56, 64, 80
guidelines for submission, 64
guilty, 83

H

health, vii, ix, x, 12, 45, 46, 49, 53, 55, 62, 63, 65, 72, 75, 76, 77, 78, 80, 81, 82, 83, 84, 85
health care, 75, 83, 85
health condition, 65
health information, 78
health systems, 63
healthcare authorities, 50, 53, 56, 63, 67
healthcare systems, 52
human, ix, 2, 3, 5, 8, 9, 12, 14, 17, 18, 19, 20, 21, 27, 41, 45, 47, 48, 49, 53, 57, 61, 72, 74, 75, 80, 85
human activity, 12
human body, 85
human dignity, 14
human existence, 12
human health, 75
human interactions, 41
human nature, 3
human subjects, ix, 45, 47, 80
humanism, 4, 7
humanitarianism, 3

I

ideal, ix, 7, 10, 25, 30, 31, 33, 36, 40, 41
identification, 65, 66, 79, 80, 85
identity, 66, 79, 82
ideology, viii, 2
IMF, 31
income, 64
independence, 56
Independence, 56
independent consultants, 57
independent ethics, 5
individual action, 29
individual rights, 74, 84
individuals, vii, ix, x, 9, 10, 25, 27, 28, 29, 30, 31, 32, 33, 34, 35, 37, 38, 39, 40, 45,

46, 48, 54, 63, 65, 66, 68, 72, 74, 75, 76, 78, 79, 82
inequality, 32, 74
information technology, 73
informational ethics, 8
informed consent, x, 46, 47, 50, 61, 76, 78, 80
infrastructure, 75
institutions, vii, ix, 25, 27, 28, 30, 31, 32, 33, 34, 37, 38, 40, 41, 45, 46, 48, 49, 52, 53, 55, 56, 57, 59, 67
intellectual property, 77, 84
interest groups, 57
International atomic energy agency, 69
international ethical standards, 48
international relations, 27
intervention, xi, 47, 72, 79
issues, vii, ix, x, 8, 9, 45, 46, 47, 50, 52, 55, 67, 71, 76, 78, 79, 80, 82

J

juridification, 5
just society, 27
justice, v, vii, viii, 25, 26, 27, 28, 29, 30, 31, 32, 33, 34, 35, 37, 40, 41, 43, 56, 80, 82, 84
justification, 7, 9, 10, 29

L

laws, 28, 37, 39, 49, 58, 67
laws and regulations, 58, 67
lawyers, 15, 47, 55, 63
lead, 4, 9, 21, 65, 66, 73, 77
leadership, 53
legal issues, 55, 77
legal protection, 9
legal standards, 50
liberalism, 7, 10
liberation, 5

Index 91

lifeboat dilemma, 16
liver transplant, 18
local conditions, 11, 49
loyalty, 13

M

management, xi, 72, 77, 78, 81
manipulation, 47, 77
materials, 50, 64, 79, 81
media, 76, 81, 85
medical, vii, ix, x, 14, 45, 46, 47, 48, 49, 51, 52, 53, 54, 55, 56, 57, 58, 59, 62, 65, 67, 71, 74, 76, 78, 80, 81
medical facilities, 48, 53, 67
medical science, x, 71
medicine, 14, 15, 32, 47, 55, 72, 85
mental health, 20
milgram experiment, 19
mission, 12, 47
misuse, 74, 82
models, 2, 6, 9, 10, 11, 16, 18, 19, 20, 21, 80
modernism, 10
modifications, 48
monism, v, vii, viii, 25, 26, 30, 32, 35, 37, 38, 39, 40, 42
moral character, 18, 20
moral codes, 5
moral dilemmas, 3
moral justness, 11
moral relativism, 4
moral reputation, 13, 21
moral systems, viii, 1, 6, 7, 10, 11
morality, vii, viii, 2, 3, 5, 6, 7, 10, 11, 13, 15, 16, 21, 25, 26, 28, 34, 35, 37, 38, 39, 40, 42, 82
motivation, 34
multiculturalism, viii, 2, 4
Murphy, vii, viii, 25, 26, 27, 30, 31, 32, 33, 34, 36, 38, 40, 41, 42, 43

N

Nagel, vii, viii, 25, 26, 27, 28, 29, 32, 33, 34, 36, 38, 40, 42, 43
nanotechnology, x, 71, 73
networking, 75
neuroscience, x, 71, 73
new ethics, vii, viii, 2, 3, 5
normative ethics, 6, 8, 9, 11

O

operations, 80
opportunities, 10, 77, 78, 80, 85
opt out, 74
outreach, 79
oversight, 51
ownership, 78

P

participants, 19, 20, 47, 48, 49, 50, 51, 56, 59, 60, 61, 62, 65, 66, 67, 79
patients, vii, ix, 18, 45, 46, 51, 52, 53, 54, 57, 59, 65, 67, 74, 81
perfectionism, 10
perpetrators, 20
personal health data, 72, 75, 84
physical abuse, 20
physical environment, 73
physical exercise, x, 72
physical laws, 39
physical properties, 39
physical sciences, x, 71
physicians, 48, 55, 65
physics, 39, 77
policy, 46, 55, 58, 78, 79, 84
political parties, 32
politics, vii, viii, 15, 25, 26, 28, 32, 34, 35, 37, 38, 39, 40, 42

population, viii, x, 50, 72, 74, 76, 77
population size, 77
postmodernism, viii, 2, 4
potential benefits, 50, 54, 61, 62, 63
practical ethics, 9
prevention, xi, 51, 72, 83
prima facie, 31, 42
principles, ix, 10, 12, 13, 14, 26, 27, 28, 29, 30, 31, 32, 33, 34, 35, 37, 38, 40, 41, 46, 53, 56, 58, 67, 69, 80
private sector, vii, ix, 45, 84
procedures, 51, 52, 58, 59, 60, 61, 63, 80, 83
professional deontology, 2, 12, 19
professional duties, 15
professionalism, 13, 15
professionals, vii, ix, 15, 45, 46, 52, 59
project, 6, 54, 61, 62, 63, 66, 81, 84, 85
proliferation, 75
protection, ix, 45, 47, 53, 54, 56, 68, 78, 84
protocol, 53, 59, 60, 62
psychiatry, 55
public health, x, xi, 65, 72, 76, 78
public interest, 13, 74
public life, 10
public safety, 4

religious deontology, 12
reports, 64, 82
reputation, 13, 21
requirement(s), 41, 58, 59, 60, 64
research funding, 54
research institutions, 49, 52, 53, 54, 56, 58, 59
research medical institutions, vii, ix, 45, 46, 48, 55, 57, 67
research protocols, 48, 51, 53, 57
research study, 48, 50, 60, 61, 62, 63, 64
researchers, 49, 54, 56, 57, 64, 65, 67, 68, 73, 76, 78, 80
resolution, 46, 52
resource allocation, xi, 72
resources, 35, 46, 59, 77
response, 52, 60, 62
responsibility for learning, 55
restrictions, 67, 77
rights, ix, 45, 47, 52, 54, 59, 60, 67, 78, 82, 83
risk(s), viii, 1, 14, 49, 50, 54, 60, 61, 62, 63, 66, 68, 72, 79, 80, 81, 82
role models, 6, 11, 21
rules, 6, 10, 11, 12, 13, 14, 29, 30, 33, 41, 47, 57, 77

Q

quality improvement, 52, 55
quality of life, 7, 68, 74
quantum mechanics, 39

R

rationalisation, 18
recommendations, 79, 80
regulations, 6, 58, 59, 67
regulatory agencies, 60
regulatory oversight, 84
religion, 7, 18

S

safety, ix, 45, 47, 54, 60
science, 47, 55, 56, 63, 73, 84
scientific method, 76
security, 20, 66, 80, 82, 83
self-interest, 28
sensors, 77, 79
services, 55, 75, 78
situational ethics, viii, 2, 3, 5, 6, 8, 9
situationism, 2
social group, 9, 15, 16
social identity, 65
social institutions, 27

Index

social justice, 41
social network, viii, x, 72, 75, 76, 81
social relations, 82
social roles, 11, 16
social workers, 55
society, viii, x, 4, 9, 17, 27, 28, 29, 30, 32, 34, 54, 57, 63, 72, 73, 74
software, 8, 77
solution, 17, 21, 41, 46, 62
sovereign state, 27, 29, 33
sovereignty, ix, 25, 28, 32, 33, 36
special ethics, vii, viii, 1, 8, 11, 12, 14
specialisation, 17
stability, 28, 82
stakeholders, 55, 63
standing operating procedures, 64
state(s), ix, 4, 5, 25, 27, 28, 29, 31, 33, 41, 68, 81
storage, 66, 67, 75, 82, 83
stress, 49, 61
structure, 26, 28, 29, 56, 84
supervenience, v, vii, ix, 25, 26, 35, 36, 37, 38, 39, 40, 41, 42, 43
surrogates, 52
surveillance, 4, 48
sustainable development, 8
Switzerland, 68, 69

T

techniques, 4, 55
technological developments, 84
technological progress, 10
technological revolution, 75
technology(ies), viii, x, 4, 8, 71, 72, 73, 74, 77, 78, 79, 80, 81, 83, 85
telecommunications, 76

threats, 5, 65
tissue, 53, 54, 69
tissue establishment, 53
tissue transplantation, 54
training, 14, 47, 50, 55, 67
transformations, 74, 80
transparency, 53, 77
treatment, 54, 56, 57, 65, 68
trial, ix, 45, 47, 53, 54, 56, 57
trolley problem, 16, 17
trustworthiness, 19
truth, 3

U

underwriting, 54
United Kingdom, 47
United States, 41
utilitarianism, 7, 18

V

valuation, 17, 18
values, 4, 5, 7, 8, 10, 16, 34, 53, 58
victims, 14, 20, 21, 41
violence, 4, 19, 65
virtue ethics and role models, 2, 10, 11, 16, 18, 19, 20, 21

W

web, 75, 81, 83
welfare, 59
well-being, ix, 45, 47, 54, 60, 84
world health organization (WHO), 47, 49, 50, 51, 57, 59, 61, 62, 63, 64, 67, 68, 69